# Expect

## Living a Life of Excellence

John Hawkins

SPEAK IT TO BOOK

**Speak It To Book**
**www.speakittobook.com**

**Expect Greatness / John Hawkins**
ISBN-13: 978-1-945793-19-6
ISBN-10: 1-945793-19-8

*This book is dedicated...*

*To my wife, Tammy, who is a daily example of what greatness and excellence look like. You're a rock star for setting the bar so high!*

*To my daughter, Sophie, who has all the potential in the world. Dream BIG, girl, and aim for the stars!*

*To my mom, who gave me a powerful foundation from which to jump off. I wouldn't be the man I am today without your love, guidance, wisdom, and direction through the years.*

*To all the family and friends who have encouraged me, challenged me, accepted me, loved me, poured into me, and taught me what Greatness truly is. Thank you!*

*Finally, this book truly is dedicated to you, the reader. I hope the insights, the stories, and especially the questions help you grow better, stronger, and faster—and to live a life of real greatness and incredible excellence.*

*Let's do this!*

*SDG Always...*

*John*

# CONTENTS

Note from the Author ................................................ 3

What You Became When You Grew Up ............................... 5

Living for a Legacy ............................................. 13

Starving at the Banquet ........................................ 31

Living the Dash ................................................ 45

Staying the Course ............................................. 59

Words Have Power ............................................... 77

Excellence Buys You Freedom .................................... 97

Plus One ...................................................... 113

Be the Diamond ................................................ 131

How to Change the World in Three Simple Steps ............. 145

Never Give Up ................................................. 161

The Next Step ................................................. 173

Notes ......................................................... 177

About the Author .............................................. 178

About Speak It To Book ........................................ 180

# Note from the Author

Thank you for picking up *Expect Greatness*!

Even though we all have different backgrounds, hopes, dreams, goals, and ambitions, every one of us is called to live a life of excellence. We are meant to expect greatness from ourselves and those around us.

As you read, you will find that each chapter stands on its own, as well as fitting into the greater mosaic of life. The workbook section after each main chapter includes reflective questions and application-oriented "action steps." These questions and action steps are meant to guide you toward a life full of success and real significance.

The workbook sections can be used for independent reflection, discussion with a friend, or group study. In addition to the spaces provided to record your responses to the questions, each chapter concludes with a page for jotting down thoughts and other notes.

Regardless of your particular reason for choosing this book, I hope that reading it will motivate, equip, and transform you as you start to expect greatness from yourself and those around you!

— *John Hawkins*

## *Free Download!*

**How To Be A Real Influencer**

*Get my free report on the simple hacks you can use every day to make you more influential at*
*http://expectgreatnesstoday.com/get-bonuses.*

INTRODUCTION

# What You Became When You Grew Up

*So we keep on praying for you, asking our God to enable you to live a life worthy of his call. May he give you the power to accomplish all the good things your faith prompts you to do.* — **Philippians 2:3-4 (NLT)**

Think back to when you were a kid. What was it that you thought you were going to be when you grew up? A fireman? A doctor? An astronaut? The president? Whatever it was that you hoped to become, it was probably something that you thought was pretty amazing. You had no trouble picturing yourself as a star athlete or singing to a sold-out concert hall. You expected your life to be great. All of your dreams would come true, and you would leave your mark on this world in a way no one could deny.

Then, as you embarked on your adult life, you nurtured aspirations of great success—maybe as a life-saving doctor, a trailblazing entrepreneur, or a world-traveling corporate executive. You dreamed of impacting lives.

What happened?

Somewhere along the line, you may have experienced setbacks. Perhaps you slammed suddenly into a brick wall of unexpected difficulties, or maybe you slowly began to drown in the humdrum details of a mundane existence. As a result, you lost some of your former spark.

You stopped expecting greatness of yourself. You ceased believing you were going to do something that would impact the world. Without realizing it, you began to hit the snooze button on the alarm as many times as possible before dragging yourself to the shower, then to work, then home again. Now you expect bills and headaches. You've lowered your standards and become accustomed to mediocrity.

Maybe somebody told you that this is just part of growing up and facing reality. Over time, you've come to believe that an average, ordinary life is all there is, and you've stopped hoping for more. Now you think it's normal to be stuck in a job you hate that's going nowhere. You convince yourself to muddle through, hoping that one day you can retire.

I am here to tell you that you are meant for more than this. You are meant for greatness.

## *Beyond Success*

What do I mean by 'greatness'? Do I mean that you are destined to ride around in a limousine from one extravagant party to the next, be greeted by screaming fans everywhere you go, and sleep on a mattress stuffed with one-hundred-dollar bills?

All of that might sound like fun, but it's not true greatness. True greatness is not about you.

If you live for your own pleasure and glory, you may enjoy yourself for a time. But when your time is up⁻ what will any of it matter? What difference will you have made?

If you want your life to be more than a flash in the pan, you need to understand that your greatness is not defined by your success but by the success of the people around you. Living life with greatness means seeking out ways to impact the lives of others. It requires intentionally seeking out people who need help or encouragement and living for something beyond personal gratification. When you expect this kind of greatness of yourself, you enable others around you to live greater lives, too.

It's tempting to confuse true greatness with worldly success. I see people, especially in the business world, who make huge sales or an enormous amount of money and don't find any greatness in it. Being able to surpass a goal is a good thing, but it isn't the same as greatness.

I often talk to people about how to be motivated, equipped, and transformed to live their best lives. My greatness isn't in how many talks I give in a year or how many people hear me speak. Rather, my greatness depends on whether or not individual lives are changed. It's not about what *I* do or what *I* have done or what *I* will do. It's about how I can rouse others to experience real success.

If I look back on my life when I am an old man and see someone who focused only on his own success, I will have been a failure. My greatness happens when my words help someone else become better and stronger. My greatness happens when I help others to be more successful.

## *The Microwave Mindset*

A life of lasting significance doesn't just happen by chance, and it isn't an opportunity available only to a select few fortunate souls. No matter where you are and where you come from, you can leave a legacy of greatness. But you have to put in the work. You have to be willing to invest.

I often ask people what their favorite part of their job is. I'm amazed at how many people say "quitting time" or "vacation" or, worse yet, can't think of a single thing. I then ask them why they're at that job, but I already know the answer. It's because they've lowered their expectations and have settled for what's easy and safe. They're afraid to work hard and put in the time and effort it takes to do something great.

People have become accustomed to a microwave culture. Now, don't get me wrong, I like microwaves. I like the speed. But to be honest, I don't usually like the food I get out of them. It's okay, but it's never delicious. I'm willing to settle for microwave meals, though, because I don't have the time for gourmet cooking. It's unrealistic to live with a microwave mindset—wanting everything to happen fast and with minimal effort—and expect life to be great.

Greatness doesn't happen overnight. It's a journey that takes consistent discipline, hard work, and dedication over time. Like preparing a healthy meal from scratch, personal greatness takes extra time and effort, but the results are well worth it.

## *The Grandkids Effect*

When people reach the final stage of this journey to true, lasting greatness, they experience what I call the "Grandkids Effect." I'm not a grandfather yet, but I've had lots of opportunities to observe grandparents. Raising children is one of the most difficult jobs known to mankind. It's a constant balance between impossible love and desiring to raise good children who can cope with the world.

The real test of whether a parent is a good parent or not isn't in how their children turn out but in how their grandchildren turn out. If the lessons they teach their children really stick, then their children, in turn, will pass them along to *their* children.

That's what I want to do for you. Reading this book will allow you to learn from me, which is good. I hope you learn a lot, but unless that learning prompts consistent, disciplined action, it doesn't have much value.

As you read, you're going to find places to pause and consider your life and to reflect, set goals, and make plans. I'm praying that you take those opportunities. It will be even better if you step out and make those things happen. This book will most impact your life when you take action and start yourself on the road to change. The real evidence that you have changed will be if you continue these new habits long after you're done reading and go on to use what you learn here to help others change their lives.

## *Free Download!*

## How To Be A Real Influencer

*Get my free report on the simple hacks you can use every day to make you more influential at http://expectgreatnesstoday.com/get-bonuses.*

CHAPTER ONE

# Living for a Legacy

*Do nothing out of selfish ambition or vain conceit. Rather, in humility value others above yourselves, not looking to your own interests but each of you to the interests of the others.* — **Philippians 2:3–4 (NIV)**

As I picture the reader of this book, I imagine someone who knows they need to change.

Life hasn't turned out how you expected it would. Maybe you can't get momentum in your career or you've just lost the job you've been working at for years. Perhaps things are going fine, but you find yourself asking, "Is this all there is?"

I would imagine readers of this book are looking to maximize their lives so that they will one day leave behind a legacy of which they can be proud.

That being said, I don't want you to read this book just for you. True, it's all about changing your life, becoming the best version of you, and living up to your full potential. And, yes, you're the one who's reading and will actually do the work. I do hope you arrive at the end of the book, look back and see the changes you've made, and feel satisfied. But don't start this process just for you.

## *What's Your "Why"?*

Think about when a smoker chooses to quit smoking. They know it's expensive, smelly, and causes lung disease and cancer. Even though they are aware of these consequences, few smokers choose to quit for any of those reasons. In reality, most people who quit smoking do so for someone else. Whether it's for their kids, their spouse, their parents, or even a job, the motivation for quitting is typically to benefit someone else.

This is a book of deep thought and honest reflection. It's a book of incredible action. But it's more than just a *self*-help book. There are thousands of self-help books in the world. You probably have several collecting dust on your shelf right now. Have they changed your life? Are you getting the results you want? No? Why not?

I think I know why.

You know that dragging yourself off the couch and going to the gym is beneficial, yet it can be extremely difficult to get up, grab your workout gear, and lug yourself there—unless you have a solid reason why. It's incredibly hard to stop doing something you enjoy, something that's comfortable, something that's a routine just because you know it isn't in your best interest. It's much easier and more pleasant to relax on the couch with ice cream and Netflix than to go somewhere to exercise. However, if you're going to get in shape to have a better quality of life, to be able to play better with your kids, or to live a long, healthy life with your spouse, suddenly moving off the couch and stepping into the gym becomes more important than giving in to your unhealthy routines. Your "why" to do something is more important than your "why not."

It's hard for people to change the way they are living their lives.

Everyone wants six-pack abs, but very few will consistently do the work to get them.

People want better jobs, but job searching is intimidating and often frustrating. The number of negative responses can be overwhelming.

A person may realize they need to stop hanging out with certain people. However, it's hard to let go of someone you have known forever, and making new friends is tough and takes time.

Someone might know they need to become healthy, but it's so easy to grab a pizza on the way home or get chips and cookies from the store and eat them in front of the TV.

If making changes depends on being motivated for their own sake, a person won't get far. It's too easy to stick with what they've done in the past and what feels comfortable. That's why your "why" is so critical to your long-term success!

So, don't read this book just for you. Read it and apply it for someone else. Don't just think about how *your* life will be better after this book; think about how someone else's life will be better because of it.

Your kids, your spouse, your co-workers, your friends, the people you haven't met yet who will be impacted by you—think of them while you delve into this.

The strategies in this book will change lives. Whose life will be impacted when you change yours?

## *The Four Levels of Life*

The best thing I can offer in this book are suggestions for what you need to change, starting now, so you can profoundly impact others in a positive way. Many authors write a book with a certain set of actions in mind. I'm not going to do that. I want to help you identify where you are now as well as establish goals to help you take steps toward change.

Several authorities on successful living, people much smarter than I am, have discussed and written about the different levels at which people function in their relationships and careers. I first heard Zig Ziglar share his thoughts in 1996 at a live event regarding four levels we all go through: survival, success, significance, and legacy.

The survival level is where people operate when they are trying to meet basic needs, such as food, clothing, shelter, and medical care. They live paycheck to paycheck just to make ends meet. They move to the success level when basic needs are being met and they start seeing more results from their efforts.

Once someone has achieved success, significance is the next level to strive toward. This is often the most difficult transition. On the significance level, people stop trying to be successful for themselves and instead look to add value to other people. They are usually specialized in a certain area and share their knowledge and expertise. To become truly significant, you must aim to become a person of value.

Legacy is when a person is consistently adding value to others and has gone well beyond success and significance. People on the legacy level positively impact others with long-lasting effects. Some notable examples of this include individuals as varied as entrepreneur Bill Gates, missionary Mother Teresa, and South African leader Nelson Mandela. Former Navy SEAL commander, humanitarian, and political leader Eric Greitens serves as one example of a world-changer of tomorrow.

All people operate on one of these levels and may be at different levels in different areas of their lives. The end goal is to leave a great legacy behind. However, you might not have arrived at that level yet. The journey will be different for each reader, so it's important to take time to assess which level you're operating on in each of the six key areas of your life: physical, spiritual, mental, emotional, social, and financial.

Let me give you an example. A single mom has three kids and works at an hourly, low-wage job to keep food on the table. From a financial perspective, it's not realistic for her to be living on the significance or legacy level just yet. Instead, she needs to set financial goals to move out of survival mode and into success mode so she can get to a place where she has the financial bandwidth to start thinking about other dreams.

Let's consider another example. A man named Steve wakes up in the morning and goes to work as a salesman. He makes a lot of calls on this particular day and sets a new personal best for making commissions. Steve spends his lunch hour looking at sports reports on his phone. He goes to supper with a guy he knows, and they complain about politics. Then Steve goes home to bed.

Steve spent that entire day living for his own glory and comfort. He is beyond survival and has become successful, but his life isn't significant. If he'd stayed in bed that day, no one's life would have been seriously impacted. Steve is leaving no legacy behind.

Maybe you're already successful in your career and finances. You're working a job that you could do in your sleep, but you're wondering if anyone will remember you when you're gone. If this is the case, you're ready for the transition to the significance level and eventually the legacy level. This book can help you, too.

When we transition from the top of one level, we typically go to the bottom of the next level. We must be aware, intentional, and accountable as we move between levels. We need to focus on what we can control and not on what we can't.

Advancing through the four levels to a life of greatness is a direct result of our choices, our vision, our goals, and our discipline. We make choices to design, deliver, and drive our development, growth, and results.

No matter which level you're on now, you don't have to stay there. Map out what steps you need to take to move from where you are now to where you want to be. Then diligently implement your plan. Surround yourself with coaches, mentors, friends, and like-minded people who support, encourage, and celebrate your journey.

## *Choosing Greatness*

There are two important principles to keep in mind as you strive to move beyond survival and even success to a life of significance that will leave a legacy of greatness.

### Intentional Greatness

The first principle involves intentionally pursuing greatness.

There's a fourteen-year-old girl I know named Melissa. Melissa is on the swim team at her school, which is about forty-five minutes from her house. The swim coach decided to offer optional practices at 5:30 in the morning. When Melissa told her parents that she wanted to attend these practices, they didn't expect her to be able to handle the extra hours of work. She had to promise that if she did the extra practice, she would not let her grades suffer or stop doing her chores. Melissa chose to commit to the extra swim practices because something inside of her said, "I demand greatness from myself. I will live at a higher level than what is average, mediocre, and ordinary."

If you finish reading this chapter, then set the book down and think, "This sounds like a good idea. I might try and be great sometime this week," it's probably not going to happen. The difficulties in life tend to get in the way and muddle all plans to be great. So, like Melissa, make a firm decision to expect greatness of yourself, starting today. Because years and years of "tomorrow" get here faster than you think.

But don't be discouraged that you're just now dipping your feet in the pool. You can't just swim a lap and wonder why you're not competing with the Olympians. First, you need to practice. Then you need coaching; and then comes the rewarding process of growing stronger and faster.

Tidal waves never reach the shore without first being set off by a tiny ripple. You need to make living with greatness a habit so that, over time, it can become your legacy.

This is a commitment you can make regardless of your circumstances. You won't always have the luxury of choosing life situations, but you are able to choose how you respond. It's important to start making choices that enable greatness *today*.

Be aware, however, that choosing personal greatness is not the same as competing with others.

I don't consider myself to be great when all I do is look at the guy next to me on the airplane and feel superior. That kind of thinking doesn't lead to legacy. True greatness is not about comparisons with others. Rather, it's about being the best possible version of *myself* each and every day!

Consider my friend Tony, a man who has chosen a life-style of true, unhindered greatness.

A few years ago, I was with Tony at a large church event. Tony is one of the deacons of that church, and we were working together to pass out groceries to people in need. There were bouncy houses, free hotdogs, and all sorts of fun going down.

Tony, preparing to give a talk to a huge group of people inside the church, headed into the bathroom a few minutes before taking the stage. While he and I were inside the men's room, a little boy—seven or eight years old—came in. And the boy was horribly sick, crying and wearing vomit and diarrhea all over his clothes.

Now, Tony could have left me to get help or ask someone else to tend to the boy. Not a single person would have blamed him. But instead of rushing off to give his important talk, he immersed himself in that moment and saw this little boy as someone he could be personally responsible for. Tony helped clean up the boy, wrapped him in his own jacket, then walked with him to the parking lot to find the boy's mom.

I doubt very much that Tony would look at that act and say, "Look how great I was!" In fact, I have changed his name so as not to embarrass him. Tony exudes a lifestyle that expects greatness of himself, and it has become such a part of who he is that he does selfless things without even thinking about it.

This is a lifestyle of investing in other people.

This is real, lasting impact.

This is true greatness.

So, what does this mean for you and me? How can we make our lives more about others?

One of the ways I do this is by daily identifying at least one person who crosses my path and investing in him or her. It might be talking with the hotel worker who makes the breakfast buffet and telling them how much I appreciate their hard work. It might be watching the audience when I'm giving a talk and making a point to spend a few extra minutes with someone who seems to be carrying a heavy burden. Sometimes it's as simple as connecting with a group on a conference call by laughing with them about the crazy things that occurred as I prepared for work.

You'd be amazed at how something that may seem small to you can make a huge difference in someone else's life. You may not always have the opportunity to see the results of your words and actions, but rest assured that if you are investing in other people on a regular basis, you're leaving a legacy of greatness.

## Feelings Versus Facts

The second principle to keep in mind as you pursue greatness?

Separating feelings from facts.

Think back to something embarrassing that happened to you. Now, try not to feel any emotions about it. Just think about the actual events. Difficult, yes? It's nearly impossible to look back without our weighty sentiments blocking the true facts.

People do this in all sorts of situations. Have you ever had someone confront you about something you said that hurt their feelings—even though your intentions were harmless? This occurs when someone assigns more feelings to facts than those facts truly warrant. It happens all of the time, and in more ways than one.

Say I climb out of bed in the morning and stub my toe. I go downstairs and spill coffee on my last clean shirt. At that point, a less-than-ideal word slips from my mouth. My six-year-old daughter reminds me that we don't say those kinds of words, and my wife frowns at me.

It would be easy to take those individual facts and allow them to color the rest of my day. The next twenty-four hours could spiral off into one big mess of adverse emotions.

In reality, though, those two negative events—stubbing my toe and spilling coffee—aren't that big of a deal. It's entirely within my power at that point to respond with greatness rather than react with anger.

I have the power to take control of my emotions and say to myself, "You know, it's not that big of a deal. Yes, my toe hurts. And, no, I didn't want to have to change shirts. But the things I have control over aren't going to be impacted by my sore toe and soiled shirt."

Rather than count the day as a loss, I can assess what happened and then use it to impact others. That, my friend, is the key.

As I talk to someone later that day, I can say, "Man, I stubbed my toe this morning and then spilled coffee on my last clean shirt. Has that ever happened to you?" I can use it to make a connection to someone, which is definitely one of my expectations of greatness.

Identifying facts quickly before responding with emotions will help you maintain your commitment to greatness through life's daily difficulties. It transforms your attitude in a way that improves not only your life but also the lives of the people around you.

Greatness.

Your words and actions affect other people, and choosing to use all of the resources available to you—even an experience as trivial and potentially annoying as spilled coffee—to add value to other people's lives is what brings significance to your life and a guarantee of lasting legacy.

This is paramount. Be careful about assigning feelings to certain facts. Instead, choose to assess the facts and use them to make a friend, a construction worker, a barista, a teller, a coworker, or an unassuming stranger's day better.

It's a beautiful first step of living for a legacy.

## *Free Download!*

### How To Be A Real Influencer

*Get my free report on the simple hacks you can use every day to make you more influential at http://expectgreatnesstoday.com/get-bonuses.*

WORKBOOK

# Chapter 1 Questions

**Question:** On which of the four levels—survival, success, significance, or legacy—are you currently operating? What steps will you take, starting today, to advance to the next level in one area of your life?

_____

_____

_____

_____

_____

_____

_____

_____

_____

_____

_____

**Question:** How are you aware, intentional, and accountable about greatness in your life? In what specific ways will you begin cultivating a lifestyle of greatness?

_____

_____

_____

_____

_____

_____

_____

_____

_____

_____

_____

_____

**Question:** Whom do you impact as you go about your day? How could you add value to their lives?

_____

_____

_____

_____

_____

_____

_____

_____

_____

_____

_____

_____

**Question:** When have you let your feelings get the better of you? How might your response have been different if you had focused on the facts?

_____

_____

_____

_____

_____

_____

_____

_____

_____

_____

_____

**Action:** A life of lasting significance comes from helping others. Start choosing greatness with your words and actions, being careful not to let emotions distort your responses. Focus on investing in the lives of the people who cross your path each day.

# *Chapter 1 Notes*

_____

_____

_____

_____

_____

_____

_____

_____

_____

_____

_____

_____

_____

_____

_____

_____

_____

_____

_____

_____

_____

_____

_____

_____

CHAPTER TWO

# Starving at the Banquet

Picture yourself ten years ago. Remember that kid? If you wrote a letter to that person, what advice would you give? Take a minute and think about it.

What hard-won lessons have you learned that you would love to teach your younger self? What pain could you have avoided? How could your life be better if you'd only known what to do?

I asked those questions to a group of professionals not long ago, and they were quick to respond.

"I'd save more money. I wouldn't beat myself up over my failures. I'd get a start on my dreams a long time ago," they said.

I was impressed by the wisdom they had gained through what must have been much struggle and heartache.

"So, are you living that wisdom now?" I asked them.
Silence.

I looked to my right, then swept back to the left.

Heads remained oddly still, and the attention that I'd held to that point seemed to melt into glazed stares.

I folded my hands together and breathed deeply.

"Why aren't you doing these things that you obviously know are good and true?" I asked somberly.

A few moments passed.

"Because I'm stupid," a man said.

The audience laughed.

Then he went on to add, "Dumb is uneducated, but stupid is a choice. Even though I have all this knowledge and wisdom," he said, twirling his hands around his head. "I'm choosing not to act on it. So I must be stupid." There were a lot of heads nodding and murmurs of, "Me, too. I'm pretty stupid, too."

"Okay," I said, "since stupid is a choice, what do we need to do to get un-stupid? What do we need to do today to get different results tomorrow? We must choose to go in a different direction starting right now."

## *The Feast*

The problem with most folks isn't a lack of education. Most people have been through a lot. They've seen a lot, learned a lot. They know where to go if they have questions. They have all the tools and resources they could possibly need within arm's reach using Uncle Google.

The problem is that they aren't doing *anything* with *everything*.

It's like they're sitting at a fabulous feast, buffet tables lined in every direction, and all they need to do is pick up a plate and help themselves to the food.

But they don't. They stand there hungry, doing nothing, complaining that there isn't anything good on their empty plates.

If they're not careful, they'll starve to death.

So, when the latest, greatest guru or expert comes along and offers them a half-chewed, regurgitated bite of a cupcake, they take it and think it's delicious and nutritious. All that amazing food is waiting, full of nutrients and flavor, but it's easier to take the chewed-up leftovers that someone else puts on their plates than to do the work themselves.

## The Three Problems and a Guy Named Tom

Eating someone else's leftovers is not a pleasant analogy. Yet think about how often people take up someone else's opinions instead of thinking for themselves.

And don't think this only applies to other people.

These words are for you, my friend.

I want to tell you about a guy named Tom. He's in his fifties and unemployed. Tom wants certainty that he'll be able to provide for his family until the end of their lives. He's worked in the automotive field for twenty-five years before getting laid off, and now he's lost his confidence. He doesn't even go on interviews anymore because he hasn't been called back for a second interview in months. After twenty applications, Tom's given up.

Been there?

When feeling stuck and unsuccessful, it's paramount to **first** dig into the root of the problem. In Tom's case, he needs to figure out his purpose for working and why he wants a job so badly. He isn't going to be motivated to find work unless he has a reason that fires him up every day!

Providing for his family is a motivating reason, but right now his own fear of failure is blinding him. Before he can pick himself up, he needs to shift his vision off his own discomfort to his need to provide for his family.

The **second** problem Tom must tackle is to figure out if his current work is a good fit for him. If he's employed in a job that doesn't engage his strengths, he only offers his employer his weaknesses. No wonder he's not solidifying any job offers. Tom needs to figure out what he's good at and what excites him before pursuing a job. This is true for any worthy goal. Training for a marathon may be beneficial to your health, but that doesn't mean you'll enjoy the running—especially if swimming is a much better fit for you.

Once Tom knows why he's working and what work he's passionate about, the **third** problem he must tackle is that of focused goal-setting—or lack thereof, at this point. Knowing that he's excited about sales doesn't mean he's equipped to be a great salesman. Tom needs to learn how to make his goals a reality—and that's not easy. It's much harder to take steps toward accomplishing goals than to sit and dream about them.

Tom's path will require careful thought. He'll have to stretch himself.

Sound familiar? Maybe you are like Tom. You want to change, but you don't know where to start. The reality is that "when the pain of being average outweighs the fear of being excellent, that is when we make our move to the next level."

It's time to advance to the next level, friend. This is your life. You only get one shot. There is no time like the present to start becoming the person you want to be, and I am here to help you take those steps.

## *Fueling Your Fire*

I look at kindling greatness as building a fire. Three things are necessary in the Fire Triangle: heat, fuel, and oxygen. When it comes to finding what's worth pursuing in life, those same three things are supreme.

The heat or spark comes from you. It's what you're passionate about, what gets you excited, and what you find yourself drawn to again and again. These are often hobbies, learning addictions, or the things you can't avoid doing even if you try.

But as you know, sparks are a dime a dozen and sputter without fuel. That's why it's imperative to seek wisdom before pouring your petroleum on any one particular flicking, orange glow. Because fuel—a combination of your skillsets and resources you've acquired or can acquire—creates quite a flame. And what's the point of burning if you haven't stopped to consider whether the sudden burst of heat will singe your eyebrows instead of warming you?

Finally, fire needs oxygen to be sustainable. Oxygen in this case is the people in your life, as well as your relationship with God.

Write this down: *I need solid people in my life to encourage, teach, and help me. I need to associate myself with life-givers, people who affirm me and impact my ability to work harder and far longer.*

These people will be life-giving and life-affirming, impacting your ability to work much longer. Similarly, pursuing a strong connection with God fills you with the constant energy needed to pursue dreams. Without this intimate connection to God and supportive inner circle, dreams die quickly.

It's easy to get off track in life when one of these important elements is missing. Time and again, a person's job may feel like they're missing the spark. They don't believe their work is significant. Or they might be unable to move forward because though they have the spark and the encouragement, they don't want to put in the work to make a dream a reality. This leads to fast burnout, especially when passion is sparked and fuel used but surrounding "oxygen"—people who are supposed to support—complain or point out problems with a person's goals.

Think about that spark you have. What is something you are excited about that you have yet to act on? Consider the fuel you would need to light a fire under that dream. It might require going back to school, starting a business, changing your family dynamic, or even cleaning your house. What relationships could you seek out and strengthen to add oxygen to your fire? With the right spark, fuel, and oxygen, you should expect greatness!

## *Setting SMART Goals*

I was once giving a talk to a group, and everyone was discussing what they would tell their younger selves. One woman said she would have started redecorating her house years ago. I asked her what she was going to do with that wisdom, and she replied, "Well, I'm going to redecorate my house before I retire." That was a good goal. It was a dream she'd had for a long time.

The first step to getting results is setting a goal, but identifying a goal is not the same as reaching it. The Goal Fairy wasn't going to fly over this woman's house, wave her wand, and make her dream come true. In order for your goal to become more than a pipe dream or a "maybe someday," it needs to be SMART: specific, measurable, achievable, realistic, and timely. You need to specify exactly what you want to achieve, make a realistic plan with specific steps and deadlines, and determine how you will measure your progress. This woman needed to decide on a budget and a style, choose a decorator, and begin working from a timeline and schedule.

I asked the woman when Christmas would be. She shot me a confused look and replied, "December 25."

I asked when we could expect Halloween. She said, "October 31."

Then I asked, "When is your yard sale to kick-start your redecorating?"

If we don't put tasks on our calendar, they don't get done!

Her face brightened. Then a co-worker volunteered to help her paint, and another said she'd go shopping with her. Before long the woman had a group of people to help her reach her SMART goal and to keep her accountable.

I'm going to give you an assignment. First, spend time identifying one of your SMART goals. Think it through and choose something you really want to accomplish. Make sure to choose just one goal. More than that can be too overwhelming and cause you to stall out.

Next, think about the specific steps you can take to meet that goal. Maybe you'll see a clear pathway of what needs to be accomplished to make it all the way to the end. Perhaps you aren't sure and your first step needs to be sitting down to coffee with someone who can help you figure out where to start. Maybe you need to find some extra work to fund this dream of yours.

Then find people to help you stay motivated. Tell your spouse, involve your kids, ask a friend to go with you, or set a date with a colleague to report back on your progress.

It's a long journey toward leaving a legacy, but the banquet is all around you. You've been living off the chewed-up remains of someone else's dreams and thinking that it was enough for a long time. Now that you know you want to eat from the banquet, you're going to have to fill your plate for yourself.

Decide on a SMART goal, identify the first step, find an accountability partner who will encourage you to succeed, and set a date for accomplishing that goal. If you want to change your life, you're going to have to choose to do the work. You have everything you need to live your best life, so stop settling for less than greatness!

## *Free Download!*

**How To Be A Real Influencer**

*Get my free report on the simple hacks you can use every day to make you more influential at http://expectgreatnesstoday.com/get-bonuses.*

# Chapter 2 Questions

**Question:** What hard-won lessons have you learned from experience that you would like to teach your younger self? What pain might you have avoided with these lessons?

_____

_____

_____

_____

_____

_____

_____

_____

_____

_____

_____

**Question:** Are you living with wisdom now? What changes have you made in light of your past experiences? What is a lesson from your past that you have yet to implement or apply fully in your life?

_____

_____

_____

_____

_____

_____

_____

_____

_____

_____

_____

**Question:** What is your spark that inspires you? What is your fuel to keep you moving toward your goals? Who is the oxygen in your inner circle?

_____

_____

_____

_____

_____

_____

_____

_____

_____

_____

_____

**Question:** What is one of your SMART goals? Be very specific and laser focused. What is your target date for achieving this goal? What first step will you take today?

_____

_____

_____

_____

_____

_____

_____

_____

_____

_____

_____

_____

**Action:** Choose to learn from your past experiences and live with wisdom now! Identify the spark, fuel, and oxygen necessary to build a fire under your dream. Pinpoint one goal you want to accomplish and figure out the first steps for achieving it. Set a date for achieving your goal and find a partner to keep you accountable.

# *Chapter 2 Notes*

_____

_____

_____

_____

_____

_____

_____

_____

_____

_____

_____

_____

_____

_____

_____

_____

_____

_____

_____

_____

_____

_____

_____

_____

_____

_____

_____

CHAPTER THREE

# Living the Dash

Years ago I was in the U.S. Navy. One day a helicopter went up on a training mission with a bunch of sailors and marines on it. I was supposed to be on the helicopter with them, but a guy named Nick went up instead because he knew I was exhausted. It had been a long evolution, and we were all worn out.

That helicopter went up about a hundred feet, flipped over, and crashed. Several people on board were killed, including Nick, who had taken my place.

## *The Beginning of My Dash*

That night I found a quiet spot looking out over the ocean. The water was so smooth that it was like glass. I vividly remember the ocean breeze, the star-filled sky, and the reflection of the moon on the water. Even in that moment of horrific loss of extraordinary men and brothers, I could see wonderful things still existed in the world.

I had good memories of Nick. He was an incredible guy whose impact went far beyond his time in the military. He had a new baby he'd never met and a wife he couldn't wait to see again. He was good at his job—really good—and had earned respect for himself from his peers and leadership. As I reflected on his incredible life and his sudden loss, one thought I kept returning to was how his death was going to affect his family.

It was during this time of huge sorrow and loss that I realized I had two paths to choose for my life. I could pursue success in the professional world, work for money, and devote myself to building up my own image. *Or* I could find out what mattered most and become a man I could be proud of. I could fill my own plate at the banquet and do truly significant things for reasons that mattered with people who mattered to me.

As I sat there, looking out at the ocean, I thought of what Nick's legacy would be—his family, his delight in his work, and his love of life were what mattered most to him. That's when I started to understand what it means to live the dash.

## *Defining the Dash*

If life were a race, most people would probably agree that it's a marathon. You're in it for the long haul, and you have to pace yourself to finish. So you save your energy for the times that matter most and slog through mile after mile of hard road. After all, look at all the years ahead before you'll reach the finish line.

Nick's life disproves the marathon ideology.

Life is oftentimes like the fifty-yard dash. It's a sprint. We need to give it everything we have, knowing that the finish line isn't miles away, but right around the next bend.

Now, I don't want to try and convince you that you should have a gloom-and-doom outlook on life. Quite the opposite, in fact. Choose to see your life as full of important moments that must not be overlooked.

We need to learn to forget the past, plan for the future, and, most importantly, be fully involved in the present.

If you knew that a loved one was going to die soon, would you look at your time differently? Rather than sitting in the car with them on the way to the grocery store in silence and letting your mind wander, you would relish the time together as precious. You might reach over and hold that person's hand and marvel at its warmth. You would try to memorize your loved one's profile and say significant things to help the person know you love them.

You don't know how long your dash will be. You might live to be ninety-eight. You might have an accident tomorrow and lose the ability to move your legs. Your job might be cut next week. Choosing a marathon mindset assumes life will continue the same for many years to come. But this view leads to complacency and a mediocre life because you believe there will be time to make changes tomorrow.

Choosing to live the dash, however, means living with passion and saying "no" to things that don't have lasting value so you can achieve a life of excellence and greatness. Living the dash means spending your time, effort, energy, and resources on those people and things that matter most to you.

A marathon mindset looks at the miles ahead. It sees the enormous potential for accomplishment and believes you can figure out and achieve what you love most somewhere down the line. But if you only have fifty yards to run, each second is crucial. The things that matter most come into laser-sharp, crystal-clear focus.

So, what is it that you want to accomplish now, starting today?

## *Planning Your Dash*

If you're going to make every day significant and leave a lasting impact on this world with the one life you are given, you need a plan to make it happen.

People often tell me their goals and then act surprised when I ask them how they're going to achieve those goals. They tell me they want to visit twenty countries in their lifetime, but they don't know where they'll start, how long they'll be there, what they want to see, or even how to obtain passports.

This happens all the time with New Year's resolutions. If you want to lose thirty pounds by changing how you eat but have no specifics to back up your intention, that's not a plan at all.

Successful people make plans, set schedules and deadlines, then execute the steps to make the plans a reality. If the idea doesn't work, they evaluate the process and adjust as needed. This is why professional athletes and other high-performing teams practice over and over and over again. Failure is a part of the process, not the end of the road.

Greatness is not something that happens by accident. Rather, it's accomplished through the successful completion of a series of goals, steps, and objectives over time.

Be aware, intentional, and accountable for your own life. Find the significance in every moment so you know that, no matter how much or little time you have, you will leave a legacy that means something.

## *The Number One Reason People Don't Live the Dash*

Maybe you've been sidelining your dreams and putting off your goals for a long time. If so, you need to ask yourself, "What is keeping me from doing something that really means something?"

A lot of the time, the answer is fear—fear of making a fool of yourself, fear of the unknown, fear of being uncomfortable, fear of being rejected, and the biggest fear of all: the fear of failing.

Too many people have never learned to push through their fear. Fear creeps into their thoughts, paralyzing them. It's a very real thing. The Bible talks about fear and what the believer's response to fear should be more than three hundred times.[1] The psalmist wrote of his response to fear, "When I am afraid, I put my trust in you. In God, whose word I praise—in God I trust and am not afraid. What can mere mortals do to me?" (Psalm 56:3–4 NIV).

I'm not going to try and talk you out of your fear. It's a heavy factor and should be treated with respect. I am, however, going to ask you to think about what would happen if you acted *in spite of* your fear.

After Nick died, it would have been easy to let fear change my perspective on life. I'd just watched a friend die, and it was tempting to say, "Well, that could have and should have been me. I guess I need to stop putting myself in risky situations because next time I may be the one who dies." It would have been easy to choose a path that took little risk and was as safe as I could possibly make it. Accepting this mindset and taking the lesser path would have resulted in lesser rewards. Giving in to fear would have kept me from greatness.

I attribute my rejection of that path to being in the Navy. You see, one of the cool things about the military is that they teach you that it's okay to be fearful, but it's not okay to let fear stop you from doing your job. Later, when I became a fireman, I was told that it's normal to be afraid when you walk into a burning building. However, it's not okay to let fear cloud your judgment or hinder your ability to do something about that scary situation.

I want you to try a little exercise. Go ahead and make a list of ten things that you fear will happen if you attempt your SMART goal. Examples include: What if I mess it up? What if it turns out I'm terrible at this? What if I fail? Write those fears down. Be specific.

Now, list ten things that will happen when this dream comes to fruition and you are successful. I can't even begin to guess all the things that might transpire if you achieve your goals. The possibilities are too amazing even to begin to record here. Again, be specific. I think you will find that it's easier to make the first list than this one. Our minds often gravitate toward what could go wrong if we fail versus what could go right if we succeed.

But if we're going to live the dash, we need to kick fear in the teeth and not allow it to control us!

Several events have occurred in my life because I seized the moment and chose greatness over fear. First was climbing Mount Fuji when I was stationed in Japan. It was a once-in-a-lifetime, truly awesome experience to see the utter magnificence of the world from the top of that mountain.

Another defining moment in my dash was when I talked to a beautiful woman in a bar who had a boyfriend at the time. I kicked fear in the face (not the boyfriend) and talked to her. Eventually that beautiful woman agreed to be my wife. Years later, we are still together, living our collective dash.

Every week I listen to people who are feeling lost and confused. Their lives are messy, full of noise and chaos. I live out my dash with greatness by helping them find the purpose in their lives.

It was daunting to climb that mountain alone. It was scary to risk rejection when I talked to that woman in the bar. And it's terrifying to challenge people's beliefs, but the rewards from living out my dash have been beyond my wildest dreams.

Circle back to the list you created of what might happen when you are successful and achieve your goal. Think about my friend Nick. His life was full of energy and purpose, and his dash, though short, will never be forgotten.

It's time to choose whether you're going to put off your life of greatness for another day in the hopes that your life is a marathon—or if you will commit to living the dash.

It's time to start giving this life everything you have.

It's time to live fully in every moment and expect a new level of greatness from yourself and those around you.

## *Free Download!*

### How To Be A Real Influencer

*Get my free report on the simple hacks you can use every day to make you more influential at http://expectgreatnesstoday.com/get-bonuses.*

WORKBOOK

# Chapter 3 Questions

**Question:** Do you spend your time, effort, energy, and resources on the people and things that matter most to you? How will you start making each day significant?

_____

_____

_____

_____

_____

_____

_____

_____

_____

_____

_____

_____

**Question:** What goals do you want to accomplish today (versus in the long run)?

_____

_____

_____

_____

_____

_____

_____

_____

_____

_____

_____

**Question:** If you knew that your time with a loved one was short, how would you treat them differently? How would you spend your moments together?

_____

_____

_____

_____

_____

_____

_____

_____

_____

_____

_____

**Action:** Live the dash! Choose to see life as full of important moments that must not be overlooked. Live each day with passion, honing in on those things that matter most. Don't get sidetracked and don't procrastinate!

# *Chapter 3 Notes*

CHAPTER FOUR

# Staying the Course

Direction and momentum, not intention, determine our destination.

When I was in the Navy, I learned about the importance of having a navigator. You see, Navy ships and submarines sail the ocean, protecting our great country twenty-four hours a day, seven days a week, 365 days per year. One group of men and women goes to sleep while another group takes over to keep the ship going. It can be days, weeks, or even months before a ship or submarine reaches its destination. Therefore, it's vitally important for the navigator constantly to check that the vessel is following the correct course to arrive at its port. There are no landmarks at sea, so this means the navigator must effectively use his compass during the voyage.

With this imagery in mind, one of the questions I ask people is, "What's your compass?"

Your compass is a combination of the people who impact you and your personal set of core values. You need to check your compass and direction continually to ensure that your life is on course. Are you living by what you say you believe, or are you letting yourself be blown around and swayed by whatever storms happen in your life?

The journey to greatness is different for every person, and your specific destination won't look the same as mine. It is imperative that you be intentional about framing who you are, what you value, and how you will live your life so you end up where you want to go.

The first step is to define your core values and create a personal creed.

## *Defining Your Personal Creed*

I am the oldest of three boys, and I spent the early years of my life living in a trailer park. We were poor, although I didn't realize how poor until much, much later.

This was a major defining season in my life.

After my father died when I was just a young boy, my mom worked several jobs to make ends meet. That wasn't an easy task with three growing boys. You'd think that the numerous people we knew (none from the trailer park) who had money would have stepped up and helped a widow with three young boys. This was not always the case. People of means could have stepped up, but they didn't.

But that's not the point of the story. The real impact and influence on my life was how my mom was always kind and serving others who were struggling, even while we were living in a trailer and having trouble meeting basic needs. Although the people of influence and means infrequently helped us, my mom was never critical or angry with them.

Confused, I once asked my mom why she was helping others when we needed help ourselves. She said, "It's important to do the right thing even when it's hard and even when no one is watching. Remember, John, your actions and choices are yours to make, regardless of what others do or don't do."

Her response stuck with me. It shaped my thinking. It became a foundation for my core values and something I incorporate daily into my personal creed.

Personal creeds are made up of those values that are the cornerstones and the very foundations of who you are at the deepest level. These values are stored up in your heart. They are what make you excited about certain topics, hobbies, or projects. They give reason to why you react the way you do when life becomes difficult. They are based on tangible experiences you've had and also on innate things hardwired in your brain.

Take some time to think about who or what your compass is. If you say it's your grandmother, I would encourage you to consider which of her attributes you most want to emulate.

Is your compass the Bible? Well, that's a pretty big book. Which verses do you most want to define your life?

You might have an inspirational saying as your compass or even a painting or a song. No matter what compass you see in your life, you need to define it clearly and then make sure you are staying on course daily.

I'm challenging you to take the time to sit and reflect on your life and write down your personal creed. It's a process and might need to take place over time, but it is important.

Make a conscious decision to take this powerful and necessary step toward greatness.

Now, take note: a personal creed is different from setting goals or making plans. Rather, it's what you use to decide what goals or plans you should pursue.

People are constantly bombarded by ideas of what they could do or who they could be. There are unlimited possibilities in this life, which makes it easy to lose sight of the end goal. A person steered by a personal creed doesn't hop in their car and drive away, knowing they need to be *somewhere*. Rather, they are focused and drive to a specific destination.

Defining your personal creed allows you to be hyper-focused on becoming your best self. Both personal and professional excellence are thoroughly entwined with having a strong, well-defined personal creed. So often people wing it and fly by the seat of their pants. That works for a while, but it never leads to greatness.

## *Tailor Made*

Let me put it to you this way: your personal creed is like going to the tailor and having a coat made just for you. It fits your exact shape and is the color and cut that you like best. No one else's coat is going to fit you like your tailor-made one.

Most people are bombarded by others' ideas, opinions, and suggestions, and it's easy to lose track of who they were made to be. So often people stray off track because they put on coats other people hand them. They attend colleges and study things that don't feed into the people God created them to be. They accept any job because it's what their parents want for them or because they don't know what else to do. They want to be thought of highly, and suddenly their coats don't look trendy enough, so they take them off and try to fit into fancier ones.

I see this all the time. I see executives whose work is phenomenally successful but whose personal lives are falling apart.

I see overworked people who are running themselves ragged, trying to do everything that seems good.

I see people who are slogging away at jobs they dislike.

I see people who are in relationships that are draining.

And I see people so numbed by the TV shows they watch or the games they play online that they don't even realize how far they've wandered off course.

What's the problem here? In my experience, one key ingredient that's missing is a personal creed. My personal creed clearly defines who I am, what I value, and how I will live my life. I circle back to it on a regular basis, holding it up against my work, my relationships, and my faith and adjusting accordingly. My creed keeps me from floating through life and taking whatever road seems like a good one. It draws me out of average and pushes me toward greatness.

## *Writing Your Creed*

The first step to penning your creed is to write down who you are. Again, put in writing who *you* are—not who your dad thinks you are or who you pretend to be when your boss is looking.

Focus on the positive. I'm nowhere near where I want to be, but being the best dad in the world is part of my personal creed. This is your chance to define what the very best version of yourself would be. These are lifelong values, not targets to hit, so forget about competing against anyone but yourself.

There are so many different things to consider when creating a personal creed that it might be difficult to narrow them down. I'm not talking about things that people around you value, nor do I mean things that you see are good and you'd maybe like to do. No, I want you to dig into who God created you to be. What really drives you? What makes you angry? What utterly excites and absolutely inspires you? Who do you dream of becoming?

Think back to words others have spoken to you that clicked in your brain. Maybe a teacher, parent, mentor, boss, or pastor gave you a piece of advice that has steered you well over the years. Think about those things that are nonnegotiable in your life, values or beliefs you'll never waver on. Consider the times when you've felt like everything was working right. What skill or passion or motivation were you making the most of when that happened?

My personal creed is influenced by my faith in God, the way my parents raised me, and my time in the military, just to name a few. My core values include discipline, integrity, servanthood, and humility. I have them written on a little index card I keep in my wallet, and I revisit them daily.

Before I make a big decision, I pull out that card and assess whether the action I plan to take aligns with my core values. When things happen that threaten to pull me down, shift my direction, or change my destination, I look back to my core values to stay on course. Am I living by my core values if I start cussing in my kitchen when things don't go well? Definitely not.

Now, I know some will read this and think, "That's a good idea, John. I'll do that sometime." Wrong answer.

If you don't put your phone down, grab a pen and a notebook, and put some serious thought into this right now, it isn't going to happen. Trust me, this is one of those defining moments on which you're going to fall back when life throws you a curveball.

## *A Litmus Test for Life*

Why does it matter if you have a personal creed? If you already know who you are and what you do and don't like, what's the point of sorting it all out and writing it down? Isn't that just a waste of time?

Think back to your high school chemistry class. Do you remember what a litmus test is? I'll explain here in case you missed that day.

A special strip of paper called litmus paper is soaked in a certain solution. Dipping this strip of paper into different liquids will reveal if they are acidic or basic, depending on how the strip changes color. If the strip turns red, the liquid is acidic. If it turns blue, it's basic (alkaline). There's no fooling a litmus test.

My well-defined personal creed serves as a litmus test for everything life throws at me. Say I am presented with a business proposal and need to decide if I should take it. I pull out my personal creed, hold it up, and decide if this opportunity is in line with who I am at the deepest level.

Even if it's a great opportunity that will look amazing on my resume, if it will cause unnecessary strain on my family, I'm not going to pursue it. My personal creed values my family over my work, and it helps me prioritize what work I choose to do. I filter how I treat my spouse, how I spend my money, and how I fill my time through my personal creed. The people I hang out with, what I watch on TV, what I read, even when and how long I exercise are tied to my creed as well.

After writing your creed, you might find that you need to change which people you spend time with, what charities you give money to, or how you eat. You'll likely need to do some pruning once you start evaluating your life in view of your creed, and that can be uncomfortable. Even good things might be eliminated. For instance, if spending so much time with friends (though not a bad thing) does not align with your commitment to prioritize your spouse, you may need to readjust a bit. It's important to remember that the short-term pain will produce better fruit in the long run.

Without litmus paper, scientists find it harder to identify if something is acidic or basic. Of course, if it's extremely acidic, it's obvious. But there's a range in the middle where it's difficult to tell. And if you aren't paying attention, what once seemed clearly acidic might seem less so because you may have become used to it. Before long, you'll find you have compromised the values you set forth in your creed, and may have even found yourself in "acid territory." You may find yourself spending time where you shouldn't, making decisions that don't align with your values, hanging out with the wrong people, or slowing in your progression toward set goals.

King David experienced this shift in values in II Samuel.

David was God's chosen king of Israel and the beloved war hero of the entire nation. But, over time, things changed in David's heart. He sent his soldiers off to risk their lives in battle while he stayed home where it was safe and comfortable. While his army was away fighting and his soldiers dying, David spied one of his general's wives and had an affair with her. Bathsheba found herself pregnant, and David—now far from his true self—went so far as to send her husband into a risky battle situation so he would be killed.

David lost sight of who God made him to be and committed both adultery and murder.

## *The Traps*

Like David, you have the propensity to fall prey to so many booby traps in this world. Those traps are waiting to woo you away from your path to greatness.

Trust me, I know.

Recently I found myself exhausted and feeling like I was spinning my wheels but getting nowhere. I was working far too many hours, but I wasn't working on the right things. Opportunities came up, and I would grab them and cram them into my already overstuffed schedule. Part of my personal creed is God first, family second, country third, work and everything else fourth. I stopped focusing on my creed—and without realizing it, work became number one and everything else was fighting for second place.

When I finally stopped and reflected on why I felt like things were off, I was shocked by what I saw. I had always thought of my personal creed as a solid oak tree that was a mainstay in my life. Somehow, I'd allowed my life to become overgrown and ridiculously unmanageable. I needed to do some pruning fast. I needed to quickly and politely remove myself from the obligations, projects, habits, and commitments that did not serve my God-given purpose.

How had this happened? I know that it started with distractions.

My personal creed dictated how I spent my time, but I had begun to make exceptions and had grown lazy. My email inbox was filled with hundreds of podcasts and blogs that I'd subscribed to over time. I had books piling up that someone else told me I should read. I was making appointments left and right to help anyone who asked. These were all good things, but they weren't in line with my personal creed. Thus, they had become weeds and dead branches that were keeping me from being my best.

When I finally decided to be serious about getting back on track, I started by listing all my commitments (312 at the time) and analyzing whether they were in line with my personal creed or not. I found a huge whiteboard and listed everything I had on my plate. I noticed that some opportunities to which I was agreeing weren't helping me to be a person of honor, courage, or commitment.

I was being asked to talk to groups about areas other than leadership. Leadership is who I am and what I am about. I live, breathe, eat, sleep, and dream about leadership. I should have gracefully declined speaking engagements that were about topics other than leadership.

Then I looked through my email and unsubscribed from everything that wasn't specifically in line with feeding my personal creed. I found loads of good podcasts and blogs, but there isn't time in the day for everything. By the time I was finished, I had brought the email subscriptions down from over 600 to 22 and cut from 228 podcasts down to 12. Good stuff doesn't make God stuff happen. I had to ruthlessly streamline my life so that I could clearly focus on God's purpose for me.

## *Tips for Success*

Now that you can see that creating a personal creed is valuable, let me offer three tips to help you to experience greater success.

First, write your creed down.

Second, find ways to reflect.

Third, have an attitude of gratitude.

Writing things down is always more powerful than thinking them or saying them. When something is written down, it is permanent and undeniable. I can't go back in time and write something different. Personal creeds should be revisited often, and bits of them will change as you change. However, putting your personal creed in writing is a strong starting point. I urge you to write down your creed and put it where you will see it on a regular basis.

Once you have written your personal creed and put it where you will see it, you need to reflect on and refine it constantly.

It's important to go one step further and give others permission to hold you accountable to your creed. Share your creed with a spouse, your best friend, or someone else you trust. Allow these people to help you use your creed to make decisions. When your behavior isn't matching your stated values, these trusted few will redirect you to the right path. If I want to prune my life well, I need someone who is farther away to help me see what I can't see up close. In the same way, other people may see your good or bad decisions more clearly than you can.

Finally, it's important to have an attitude of gratitude.

Too many times when people are setting goals and objectives, they forget to be joyful in what they currently possess. They might look at what they are not and what they don't have. There's a real tendency to become mired in how much work is ahead. If this happens, consider taking two steps back for every one you take forward, but focus your gratitude on the forward steps every time you take them.

Creating a personal creed will ensure you stay on a path that reflects your true self. This creed will become a powerful tool in your life, one you will begin to lean on more than you realize.

When something tough comes up, you can look at your compass and choose not to fail. As situations arise that, in the past, would have tempted you to stray from your core values, your creed will hold you firm and help you deflect any distractions or obstacles that come your way.

With focus and determination, you can deliberately guide your life on a sure course to greatness.

## *Free Download!*

### How To Be A Real Influencer

*Get my free report on the simple hacks you can use every day to make you more influential at http://expectgreatnesstoday.com/get-bonuses.*

WORKBOOK

# Chapter 4 Questions

**Question:** What are your core values? Be specific and limit to six or seven. If you choose too many, it can become overwhelming. The U.S. Navy uses three: Honor, Courage, and Commitment. I use four: Discipline, Integrity, Servanthood, and Humility (My personal D.I.S.H).

_____

_____

_____

_____

_____

_____

_____

_____

_____

_____

_____

_____

**Question:** What or whom do you need to prune from your life today in order to align with and stay focused on your core values?

_____

_____

_____

_____

_____

_____

_____

_____

_____

_____

**Question:** What elements in your life are trying to distract you from your core values? What specific steps will you take to remove or avoid these distractions and stay on track?

_____

_____

_____

_____

_____

_____

_____

_____

_____

_____

**Action:** Create a personal creed to ensure you stay on a path that keeps you in line with your core values. Here is your assignment:

- Set aside time to reflect on your personal creed. Make a list of things that matter most to you and try to understand your core values. Consider what *your* best self would be (not your dad's best you or your spouse's best you). Remember, this is a work in progress. The most important thing is to start.
- Once you feel that you have a personal creed that represents you well, write it out and put it where you will see it daily. Keeping it in your wallet is fine, but ask yourself if you will pull it out and look at it regularly if it's in there.
- Identify someone who can help you stay true to your personal creed. Give that person permission to call you on things that aren't in line with who you want to be. Part of giving permission is also extending grace. You might feel hurt or become angry or frustrated when this person points out that you have drifted off course. Allow yourself to feel hurt or angry for a minute. Then extend grace to yourself and your accountability partner and move on.

## *Chapter 4 Notes*

CHAPTER FIVE

# Words Have Power

A while back I was talking with Dave, a powerful executive in a big company. He started disclosing how his boss liked to micromanage him. As I chatted more with Dave, he realized he was living in fear. He was afraid of speaking up and losing his job. He was afraid of not being able to provide for his family. Dave shook his head and said, "When I was twenty years old, I was unstoppable. Now I'm forty-five, and I'm afraid of my own shadow. What happened?"

Somewhere along the way, someone likely spoke words of doubt or negativity to Dave that settled in Dave's mind and heart. Those seeds of doubt or negativity slowly began to grow and spread, impacting Dave's thoughts about himself. Eventually, they grew into a vast forest of withered, poisoned trees.

I shared with Dave that without realizing it, he had grown to believe those untruths, and they had become his reality. Now all he had was a tiny axe to cut down this massively huge forest of untruths.

Dave thought about that for a minute and then said, "On his second day, my new boss told me that for someone in my position, my performance needed to be substantially higher. I took that and magnified it in my head and have been walking on eggshells for the past four years. Now my blood pressure is high, my relationship with God is non-existent, and I feel like I'm losing my family."

As we talked, Dave began to see his difficulties originating from that moment when his boss's words took root in his heart. "I came home grumpy that day, and I've been grumpy ever since. No wonder my family's falling apart. It's not their fault—it's my fault," he said. "I've given room and space in my life for these words of death and fear to exist, and I'm not going to do it anymore." Sure enough, Dave quit his job soon after and found one that builds him up rather than breaking him down. His relationship with God is back on track, and his family is on solid ground again.

It's amazing how much power words have over people.

## *Words That Kill*

Once you have created a personal creed—the written document that will be a constant reminder of what your core life values are—your next step is to consider the effect others' words have had on your life.

This difficult step is necessary and critical to fighting things in your past that may be holding you back from being who God intends for you to be today.

The Bible says words can bring life or death (Proverbs 18:21). I'm confident it wouldn't take much effort for you to think back and come up with some words that have produced rotten, withered trees in your life.

Sometimes words that cause death are intentionally cruel words. Sometimes they're just words that hit you at a bad time, but are associated with something negative that wasn't necessarily meant by the one who spoke them. And sometimes the words that hurt the most you overheard or read, and they've been killing you ever since.

I think of how much damage is done to women by the media. Even young girls are constantly being told how they should look, how they should dress, and how thin they should be. These messages are being created by people who won't ever know whom they're affecting, yet they influence millions of women. By the time girls are in middle school, they've already seen thousands of ads about how to be "perfect."

It is critical that you understand how important it is to be ridiculously intentional and focused on what words you allow to take root in your life.

## *Leveling Our Poisoned Orchards*

Not all words, however, are life-taking. The power of words aptly spoken is like dynamite—they can level existing orchards of negativity if they're spoken at the right time and place.

These words of life can come from many different sources. There are times when a sermon, a motivational speaker, or a book clicks on a light bulb, and suddenly the dead trees in life are illuminated for what they are—and they disintegrate.

I'm not sure why, but there is such power in being able to clearly see the causes of things. When it's unclear where the original negative seeds came from, it's like the soil around the roots becomes too strong. But by digging in and examining the first planting of words of death, those words often lose their power.

One of the best ways to destroy withered, dead orchards is by reading about what God has done for you and how He feels about you. Get out your Bible or your Bible app and read Psalm 139. I especially like how the New Living Translation puts it: "How precious are your thoughts about me, O God. They cannot be numbered! I can't even count them; they outnumber the grains of sand!" (Psalm 139:17–18 NLT).

Talk about words with the power to destroy words of death!

If God—who created the universe, who made atoms, who thought up the creatures of the deepest ocean—thinks about you more often than there are grains of sand on the earth, how infinitely precious you must be! Any stupid, thoughtless words that might have been spoken by mere humans fade away in comparison to the unshakable love of Almighty God.

## *The Right "Why"*

Of course, there are areas in every person's life where the words of death don't go down easily. There are words that have taken such root that they can only be pulled up with diligent work, maybe over several years. When you hit those areas of your life, and when deep-rooted negative beliefs won't go away, it might seem like God's truth doesn't really have that much power. "They're just words. This whole concept is just a gimmick," you might say to yourself.

For some reason, words of death burrow into the soil of a person's heart easily and sprout quickly. They take hardly any tending at all before they speedily propagate into fully grown trees producing poisonous fruit.

Conversely, words of life require fertile soil and plenty of nurturing to produce healthy fruit. They need action to benefit a person at all. Since it takes so much effort, it is easy to believe God's Word does not cause change.

Like any other difficult, long-term change, removing words of death and planting words of life requires the right "why."

Pretend you're in line at the post office. You've waited twenty minutes, and the lady on her cell phone behind you is driving you nuts. All you want to do is mail your package and run to your car.

In comes a guy who asks if he can go to the front of the line. All fifteen people in that line glare at him and tell him to wait his turn. There is no reason why he should be allowed to go ahead of them. But then the man explains that his daughter who has cancer is waiting in the car. She is on her way home from the latest round of chemo. He says she can't wait in the heat for long. Every person in that line is quick to tell him that he should absolutely go first.

You see, with the right "why," people are willing to endure difficult, even painful, experiences cheerfully.

I talk to a lot of people who tell me they want to make a million dollars. When I ask them why they want a million dollars, I often receive the same response: "Because then I will have truly 'made it' in this life." If I ask what specifically people will do when they reach this goal, they say things like, "I'll pay off my debt. I'll travel. I'll get a new car." But none of these reasons is a good enough "why" to motivate anyone, nor is the arbitrary goal of a million dollars built on anything lasting.

In the same way, people may attend conferences to listen to motivational, inspirational speeches, but then they do nothing about it when they get home. They don't apply a single thing that they heard long-term, and the post-conference high typically doesn't last for more than five days or so. The positive feelings they experienced don't last long enough to knock down any of that dead forest of doubt and fear. In fact, fear of failure and rejection often snuffs out enthusiasm for lasting change so fast it's scary.

Ask yourself how strongly you really believe in making that million dollars.

You see, your "whys" start to fall apart at two in the morning when you're exhausted, or when you're hungry, or lonely, or angry. When my "why" is rooted in my own comfort or benefit, when it's only about me, it rarely motivates me for long.

However, when your "why" is about others, it becomes unstoppable. I've seen this in business, in the military, in sports, and in marriage. It's massive. People can do so much more when they do it for others.

I think back to Dave, who was living in fear of his boss. He was afraid that he wouldn't be able to provide for his family and used that as a reason to stick with a miserable work environment. But when Dave understood the damage he was doing to his family, suddenly he had the courage to stand up to his boss and quit his job. Losing his family was an unstoppable "why" that far outweighed his fear of standing up to his boss.

Words can defeat, or they can release power. Finding your unstoppable "why" will instill in you the courage to take up action against words that may be tearing you down.

## *Who Are You Listening To?*

When I was in high school, I was going places. I had potential scholarships on the table to several different colleges. I had been a Rotary Exchange Student to Mexico, performed numerous community service projects, and earned good grades. At the same time, I was surrounded by people who were making bad choices and going nowhere fast.

One day, my friends wanted to skip school and go mess with this guy who'd been causing them problems.

They were my friends, so I went along with them. I didn't know what they had in mind, but I was in the car with them when they threw a homemade Molotov cocktail through a window into this guy's grandmother's house. The window broke, the curtains caught fire, and her cat was killed.

Even though I was horrified by what had happened, I couldn't stop being friends with these guys. You see, I was so desperate for friends that I would have done just about anything to hang out with anyone who would give me attention. I'd been striving my whole life to be accepted, but because I made some poor choices about whom I spent time with, I ruined my chances for college scholarships.

Of the five guys who were with me that day, one is dead, two have been in prison, and one has been divorced three times and can't hold down a job. The major difference between me and those guys was a teacher, Mrs. Manley, who stepped into my life and spoke encouraging words to me when I needed to hear them most.

Mrs. Manley saw what a mess I'd made of things and took me aside one day. She told me that I had talent, ability, heart, drive, dedication, and motivation. She said I could change the world. Mrs. Manley was the first person to point out to me that my friends were holding me back from living up to my full potential.

For too long, I had been listening to the wrong words, which spoke death into my life. Mrs. Manley's words spoke life into my soul and began to uproot and destroy the forest of untruths I had allowed to form in my mind.

## *Get Your "But" Out of the Way*

It's so much easier to listen to the negative than the positive. Success sometimes feels like a lottery. There's one chance for success and dozens of chances for failures. You just hope the lucky ball will be the one you pull out.

You may set a goal and then tack on so many "but" riders that your dreams never get off the ground. You may think: I'm going to be a millionaire—

- but it probably won't be for a couple of years.
- but I must get a new job, a new wife, a new house, and a new car first.
- but I don't have the right education for it.
- but who would ever listen to me?

In my Navy training days, I often said, "I'm going to swim two miles today." It wasn't until I was a mile and a half into the swim that things got tough. My muscles screamed at me, and I was exhausted. Every part of me wanted to quit, but at that point I was still half a mile from shore and had no choice but to keep going. I would tell myself, "This is easy, you got this" and keep pushing until I was back on dry land.

I told myself I could do it, and I was right.

Of course, there were also days when I stood on the shore and looked out at the water in front of me and told myself there was no way I could make that swim. I told myself I couldn't do it, and I was right.

Success isn't as simple as picking a number out of a hat. It's about hard work, dedication, intentional action, discipline, and words of life.

Every single time you tack a "but" onto a goal, you are planting a seed of death in that dream. Every time you tell yourself you can push through the difficulty and the fear and the exhaustion, you are nurturing the seeds of life that you planted and keeping the words of death from taking root.

Now, let's be clear. There's a difference between choosing the "buts" and being realistic. When someone decides that he is going to run a marathon, he isn't going to jump off the couch and run the full distance right away. There are very real barriers that need to be dealt with to meet this goal in a healthy way. Saying to yourself, "I want to run a marathon, and I first need to research training schedules and find a running buddy," is not the same as saying, "I want to run a marathon, but I don't know how." It's wise to research, ask questions, and set smaller goals for yourself. Without those smaller actions, the bigger action won't happen.

"Buts" are deadly because they are little more than excuses to prevent you from ever taking the first step. They are rooted in fear and worry and discomfort. "Buts" look at all the work required and say, "Nope. It's too hard, and there are too many reasons why I'll fail." It's standing on the shore and seeing how far a two-mile swim really is and then deciding the result isn't worth the work.

To nurture the words of life, it is paramount that the right "why" be what motivates you. Then, surround yourself with people who will help along the way, and let go of the people who try to pull you off the right path. Finally, be vigilant about the "buts" that inevitably come along that will keep you from taking the next steps.

## *The Power of Gratitude*

There's a crucial aspect to remember regarding the power of words. Not only do other people's words have power in your life, your words have great power in the lives of others.

Now, when your words are taken out of context or given emotions that you never intended, that is not your responsibility. I'm not saying you must feel guilty for every person whose feelings have ever been hurt by things you didn't mean. However, intentionally speaking life into people's lives can be life changing.

One of the simplest ways to speak life into people's minds and hearts is to speak words of gratitude, so that's a good place to start.

Deliberately choose three people you interact with today and thank them. Don't just say, "Thanks for the coffee" or "Thanks for doing something for me." Go out of your way to tell the barista at your local coffee shop, "Thanks for getting up so early to serve me coffee." Stop and tell your employees, "Thank you for working so hard and doing this job well. Thank you for giving it your best."

Don't ask for anything. Don't correct anything. Don't make it about you. Keep it simple. Identify one specific thing. Drop the GTB (Gratitude Truth Bomb) on them, walk away, and see what happens. Start with three people today, four the next day, five the day after that, and so on.

This is a gradual, intentional process. Over time, however, gratitude will become a part of your life. It will become a part of who you are. When you approach people with gratitude, you create fertile soil where you can plant seeds of life. Without adequately preparing the soil, seeds will not take root.

Before long, that annoying co-worker who drives you crazy will be on your side because of your genuine, meaningful gratitude. Your moody teen will surprisingly want to spend time with the family without bribery. The waitress who serves your family every Friday night will start calling you by name and looking forward to seeing you.

To experience these types of results will take humility and a putting aside of the need to be superior, which is extremely tough. However, once gratitude has softened hard ground, you will be able to start speaking words of life into people around you—intentionally speaking life into people's lives will be visibly life changing. Imagine how much more productive your team, your family, and your co-workers will be when you have an attitude of gratitude.

Words are powerful beyond human comprehension. They can breathe life into a person or suffocate them to death. Cast aside any words spoken that speak death, and remove the "buts" in your life that are preventing you from moving forward.

Above all, stand firm in what you have learned, for the next step may be one of the hardest to take: it's time to deal with the insatiable desire to be perfect.

## *Free Download!*

### How To Be A Real Influencer

*Get my free report on the simple hacks you can use every day to make you more influential at http://expectgreatnesstoday.com/get-bonuses.*

WORKBOOK

# Chapter 5 Questions

**Question:** What does your heart long for? And what is your real "why"?

_____

_____

_____

_____

_____

_____

_____

_____

_____

_____

_____

_____

**Question:** Who in your circle is speaking words of death? How will you completely avoid or distance yourself from these people? Who is speaking words of life? How can you interact with the positive influencers more?

_____

_____

_____

_____

_____

_____

_____

_____

_____

_____

**Question:** To whom do you need to show gratitude today? How, specifically, will you express your thankfulness?

_____

_____

_____

_____

_____

_____

_____

_____

_____

_____

**Action:** Set aside any words that speak death, and remove the "buts" in your life that prevent you from moving forward.

It's time now for you to get to work. Here are the steps I want you to take starting today!

1.  Examine the seeds that have grown into trees in your life. Think back on any words of death you've allowed to take root. Identify them and recognize the power that you've given them. Remember that your past does not define your future.

2.  Spend time thinking through your goals. What is it that your heart longs for? Why do you want these things? If your "whys" aren't strong, you won't be motivated enough to make your goals realities; negative words rooted in your mind and heart will speak louder. Find your unstoppable "whys." Then write those "whys" on index cards and put them where you'll see them regularly. When things become hard, look back at your notes and remember why the struggle is worth it.

3.  Consider the people around you who speak life-giving words. Are there people you need to distance yourself from or stop spending time with altogether? Who in your life is speaking words of death that you can't avoid? You'll need to be vigilant to weed out those negative people, and quick to dig up any seeds they toss out that will grow bad trees. These

are the people you need to spend time with and allow to nurture you.

4. Get rid of your "buts." When you look at who you want to be and what you want to achieve, stop listening to the "buts." Take those dream killers and recognize the fear that's attached to them. Then look at what reasonable, realistic steps you need to take to reach your goals.

5. Finally, choose three people you will show gratitude toward today. Remember, don't make any requests or corrections. Don't make it about you. Be specific, keep it simple, and be genuine.

# *Chapter 5 Notes*

CHAPTER SIX

# Excellence Buys You Freedom

"Nobody's perfect."

Did a parent, a teacher, or a friend ever offer you that reassuring platitude when you were younger?

Maybe they missed the thousands of TV commercials, advertisements, and magazine covers that all tout the secrets to perfection. Many mass-marketing experts want you to know that the perfect body, diet, outfit, and vacation all exist and must be pursued.

If you fall short of perfection, their ads insinuate, you're a failure.

But guess what? There's good news: whoever told you "Nobody's perfect" was a lot wiser than the commercials would have you believe.

## *The Slave Master*

The word 'perfect' is thrown around so much these days that people have stopped thinking about its impact.

People desire the perfect house, the perfect Christmas, the perfect car, or the perfect family.

Unfortunately, the repeated failure to achieve perfection then leaves people feeling unworthy and unlovable.

Perfection fascinates me. For many years, I was what you would call a perfectionist. To me, perfection was the only acceptable outcome, and I would beat myself up when I didn't reach it. Perfection is, of course, unattainable, except in certain extreme conditions and situations.

Striving for perfection is demoralizing. It will enslave you and turn every person around you into your master as you begin to believe they all see where you failed and find you unworthy. You will begin to compare yourself to people you see as superior. You will assume that everyone else is comparing you to others.

On top of that, when perfection is your slave master, you become a master to everyone else, too. You begin to compare everything you do to what others do, and you will either be left wanting or feeling superior. When a person feels superior, they like to wallow in it, looking down on everyone else while believing they are better.

Here's what I've learned about perfection: it's all about taking things away. Did you ever notice that? When I strive for perfection, I remove everything that does not contribute to my ideal. I must lose ten pounds. I need to remove the ugly décor in my home. I need to eliminate my children's bad habits. Perfectionism is a bully. It finds a person's weaknesses and then points them out again and again until those weaknesses are the only things they can see.

There is no possible way for any of us imperfect humans to be utterly perfect. Even if I managed to achieve the goal of perfection I set, there would still be something inside me that would not be satisfied. I would find myself looking back and seeing something I could have done better.

Perfection is a single moment in time that a person works toward. They may reach that evanescent moment where they achieve their goals, but then the moment fades away. They're left in the dark again, looking for another flicker of light to pursue. While those moments of achievement might be glorious, they are fleeting. The emptiness that follows is an ever-deepening hollow that enslaves the person even more.

## *Quitting Perfection*

There were two body builders I once knew. One pursued perfection. I mean, he measured every mouthful of food, counted every calorie and rep, worked out constantly, and was determined to come in first place in a major competition he entered. When he came in fifth place, this man was devastated. He curled up in the corner of the back room. His entire identity was tied up in being first and achieving perfection. Once he missed that goal, he didn't know who he was anymore.

The other body builder was driven to be excellent. He worked out rigorously and watched his diet carefully, but he never put coming in first on the altar of perfection as something to be worshiped. When his family went out for pizza, he went along and had a few slices. This man came in ninth place at the same competition as the first bodybuilder. After the awards were handed out, he walked around and talked with the other contestants. He even met Arnold Schwarzenegger. He was laughing and chatting and enjoying the entire experience.

Only the top three contestants received any sort of prize money or endorsements, so both of these men earned the same amount (nothing). But the second man walked away with so much more than the first. For him, the entire experience, not just the first-place trophy, was the goal. He sought excellence versus perfection in the competition.

It's tempting to look at perfection and believe you must pursue it, or else you're lazy. Stepping away from perfection doesn't mean your life needs to be less. To stop striving for perfection won't leave an empty void in your life.

When I made a conscious effort to stop, I was afraid. I didn't want to be sloppy or open myself to criticism from others. After all, if I'd worked that hard and still fell short, what would happen when I stopped striving for perfection?

I was surprised to find that the room in my brain and heart previously filled with my slave master's cruel dominance wasn't replaced with fear and shame. Instead, when I put my efforts toward caring for other people, my brain and heart were filled with understanding, love, and lots of grace.

## *Pursuing Excellence*

Now I put all of my energy, efforts, and resources into striving for excellence. Please hear me out. You might be rolling your eyes and dying to tell me that perfection and excellence are the same, and that I'm caught up in word play. You couldn't be more wrong.

Where perfection is a slave master, excellence buys freedom. It's a lifelong achievement, not a single moment in time. It's the difference between what you learn over the course of your entire education versus how you do on a single test.

Perfection is wrapped up in how things appear and how other people perceive you, while excellence is about how things are done and what you truly are at your deepest level.

Perfection is about doing something right; excellence is about doing the right thing.

Perfection repels, while excellence is a magnet.

The definition of 'perfectionism' is "a disposition to regard anything short of perfection as unacceptable."[2] How unrealistic and ultra-demanding! There's no way to go through life as a perfectionist and feel anything other than worthless the vast majority of the time. However, the definition of excellence is "the quality of being outstanding or extremely good."[3] Much more attainable, isn't it? I can't be perfect, but I can be unusually good. I can surpass ordinary standards.

One of the greatest benefits to pursuing excellence is how it allows you to handle failures. Perfection holds up failings and rubs your nose in them. You won't be allowed to forget shortcomings and must be motivated by fear, guilt, and shame.

On the other hand, when failures happen while you're striving for excellence, you can learn from them and allow them to help you grow. While they aren't exactly welcomed, they are expected. I will fail in everything I try on some level or another. It's not shocking and debilitating when mistakes come along because I'm a human being and I mess up. I might need to apologize, rethink things, and do some soul searching, but I can forgive myself and move on.

Excellence is also a habit, and it has no limit. Perfection is the glass ceiling, and it's exhausting. A perfectionist either spends all his time climbing toward the top of the mountain, or he's failing in his attempt. Excellence, however, sees the opportunity to improve life with every step. There is no one to compete with; no one is superior. If I run a race and do my best and come in fourth, I can be happy with myself. A perfectionist, on the other hand, might do the best they can possibly do, come in fourth, and feel like a failure because they fell short of the winner.

My best isn't my neighbor's best. Boy, is that a freeing thought! I know there will always be someone out there who is better, faster, more attractive, and smarter than I am. When I'm in excellence mode, I see those people and feel happy for them. They might spur me on to try new things, but if I never reach their level it's okay. I stop being jealous of them. I no longer feel superior to those who aren't on my level. You tried your best and came in tenth place? Way to go! Let's celebrate.

I came in fourth place—do you want to train together? I can show you my workout routine, and you can show me yours. Maybe next race we'll do even better.

So strive for excellence! You will never be left feeling "less than" or like you failed. Instead, you will experience contentment and joy in your and other people's achievements, and you will be free.

## Everyone Can Be Excellent

Perhaps you've been reading this chapter and know for certain you are a perfectionist—you're driven to absolute perfection. You might even be on the other side of the pendulum and find perfectionism repulsive. Maybe you had a parent who drove you toward perfection and you've spent your life rebelling against it. Maybe you just don't have the need to try that hard. Perhaps you're so beaten down by life that you can't bear the thought of even attempting perfection.

Here's the good news about excellence: it's for everybody. No one can be perfect, but everyone can be excellent.

Consider where you are in life right now, wherever that is. You might be struggling to jump-start anything, or you might be speeding through life, hitting on all cylinders. Wherever you are on that spectrum, you can be excellent right where you are.

Ultimately, freedom is found in excellence. It truly is. Every single step I've encouraged you to take so far is summarized in being excellent. Choose excellent words. Pursue excellence by listening well. Be motivated toward excellence with your unstoppable "whys." Live excellently so that you enjoy the feast. Live the dash with excellence. Expecting greatness from ourselves leads us to live a life of excellence. Perfectionists only find value in themselves based on what they *do*. People of excellence find value in themselves based on who they *are*.

Striving for excellence means going out and touching people's lives, encouraging them to be their best, and being boundlessly grateful. Perfection is so single-minded and finite. Excellence increases and multiplies when the people around us are also excellent. It's eternally significant, while perfection is entirely forgettable. Excellence draws people in, while perfection drives people away.

## Choosing Excellence

To check whether you are pursuing perfection or excellence, ask yourself two reflection questions: First, did you give your best? Second, did you give your all? You might think that these are the same question, but they aren't. I can give my best and not give my all or vice versa. These two simple questions help me to determine if I'm living a life of excellence, and they will help you as well.

As you go through your day, keep asking yourself, "Did I give my best? Did I give my all?" If you can answer yes to both, you are chasing excellence. Other people's reactions and opinions don't affect your excellence. If you gave your best and gave your all to a project that turned out to be a flop, you still contributed excellence. If you gave your best and gave your all to your family when you arrived home from work—even if your spouse had a bad day and the baby was fussy—your family was better for it, and you contributed excellence.

Excellence is a firm and fair taskmaster. If you begin to feel in bondage to it, you are likely sliding toward perfection and need to stop and reassess. If you are unwilling to attempt excellence, you already know what life will be like because you're living it. When you find that you are unhappy and know that life needs to change, circle back to excellence. Ask yourself if you are giving your best and your all.

God is important to me, and He fits into this discussion about excellence over perfectionism in profound ways. We can work toward excellence, but in and of ourselves, we aren't capable of achieving perfection. Only God is perfect.

God's Son, Jesus, came to earth and led a perfect life and died in man's place. He now offers His perfection to replace man's failures, but each person must reach out and take it. God can't have anything sinful near Him, which means there's no hope for anyone outside of Jesus Christ. I have found so much freedom and hope in knowing that when God looks at me, He sees His Son's perfect record because I have accepted Jesus' gift.

If your heart is crying out for freedom from guilt and shame, please start looking into the Bible's truths. They can transform your life more than anything else in the entire universe. I know because I tried just about everything, and nothing compares to the freedom I've found in Jesus.

I don't have to try to be perfect. I choose to chase excellence. My family, my work, my team, and my friends are all better because of this pursuit.

So I ask you: Are you giving your best? Are you giving your all?

You're already equipped with a personal creed and the boldness to fight off any negative speech that has prevented you from becoming who you were created to be.

Now it's time to deal decisively with the pressure to be perfect, which is trying to enslave you and make you feel unworthy. It's time to choose excellence.

## *Free Download!*

### How To Be A Real Influencer

*Get my free report on the simple hacks you can use every day to make you more influential at* http://expectgreatnesstoday.com/get-bonuses.

WORKBOOK

# Chapter 6 Questions

**Question:** What does 'perfection' mean to you? What does your perfect life look like? How can you make the transition to excellence starting today?

_____

_____

_____

_____

_____

_____

_____

_____

_____

_____

_____

**Question:** How do you handle your failures or shortcomings? How do you overcome them?

_____

_____

_____

_____

_____

_____

_____

_____

_____

_____

_____

_____

**Question:** What are several specific ways in which you can choose excellence on a daily basis this week?

_____

_____

_____

_____

_____

_____

_____

_____

_____

_____

_____

_____

**Action:** Pursue excellence by choosing your words carefully and listening well. Focus on your unstoppable "whys" to motivate yourself toward excellence. As you work to live your daily life above ordinary standards, don't forget to look for your freedom—and enjoy the feast!

# *Chapter 6 Notes*

CHAPTER SEVEN

# Plus One

There is an old joke that begins with the question: How do you eat an elephant?

The answer? One bite at a time.

Sometimes life feels like a huge elephant—an entire herd of elephants on some days—that we're supposed to eat all at once. It's easy to become caught up in the enormity of life. Sometimes it might seem easier to sit and starve rather than pick up a fork and dig in.

This is where the idea of "Plus One" comes in.

Too many people try to do too much in a month and not enough in a year. This is why most people continue to live average, ordinary, mediocre lives. It's easy to get overwhelmed when you try to do everything at once. The beautifully simple thing about the Plus One concept is that you don't have to take on the whole thing—you only need to add a little bit at a time to one area of your life.

There are six areas in life people have control over: physical, spiritual, emotional, financial, social, and mental.

You might realize that you have work to do in all six of these areas, but if you set out to change all of them at once, you're unlikely to experience lasting success. It's just too much to handle all at one time.

Instead, choose one area that needs improvement. For example, let's say you want to work on your physical self. You want to be able to do one hundred push-ups.

Maybe you can do twenty or thirty already. Maybe you can do one hundred, broken into smaller segments. Or maybe it's a challenge to do just one.

The Plus One concept says to add one more to what you are already doing. So on the first day, you add one push-up more than what you were already doing. If you were not doing any at all, you would start with one push-up.

The next day, you do two push-ups.

On the third day, you do three push-ups, and so on. And by day fifteen, you are doing fifteen push-ups every day.

Say you want to improve your finances by building your savings account. Online banking can make this a lot easier. Today you would move one dollar to savings. Tomorrow you would move two dollars to savings. The day after that, you would add three dollars to savings.

In a lot of ways, Plus One is like building your stamina. Once you've developed a healthy daily habit in one area, you can stop adding and start maintaining.

If you feel like thirty push-ups a day is where you want to be, and you're already doing them on a regular basis, choose a new Plus One in a different area while you continue to do thirty push-ups a day. You can always revisit your previous Plus One goals if it becomes necessary.

## *The Power of One*

The idea of one is so simple that it's easy to overlook. I know some reading this book will say, "Really, John? You think my life will be changed by adding one more minute? One more pushup? One more dollar to my savings account?" One is such a small number, how can it be important?

Let me put this in perspective:

I see the power of *one* negative sentence on people's lives all the time. Think about it. How often does someone say one thing that clips your wings for life?

And, conversely, one positive sentence can steer you to a new path that leads to greatness.

Have you ever watched the Olympics? Think about the power of one hundredth of a second. For some athletes, that split second is the difference between silver and gold, or between winning a medal and going home empty handed. Move one degree, from 211 degrees to 212, and water boils.

One single cup of coffee made an enormous difference in my life. While I was in the military, I went through a time when I was depressed and had suicidal thoughts. It grew so bad that I took a Sharpie and wrote my name on a bullet. I would sit and look at that bullet and know that this was the bullet that would end my life. I even went so far as to plan where I would kill myself so it wouldn't make a mess for others to clean up.

There was a guy named Joel who was an acquaintance of mine and knew a little of what was going on. One day, he asked me to go and get a cup of coffee with him. It was a little thing. It wouldn't take much time. It wasn't expensive. So I went and got a cup of coffee with Joel, and we sat and talked.

At the end of that talk, Joel asked if I would get a cup of coffee with him the next night. Every time we'd end our coffee times, he would ask me to get one more cup with him another time. Sometimes we'd talk so long we'd get a second cup of coffee and then a third. We even got kicked out of Denny's a few times.

Then the night came when I turned to him and said, "You know, I don't think I need the coffee anymore."

You see, Joel had helped me talk through so much of my past that it didn't have the grip on me that it used to. And because he only asked for one more cup of coffee, I could wrap my head around it. I could put off killing myself one more day, and then one day after that, until I didn't want to die anymore. For me, one cup of coffee was the difference between life and death.

Before I can build a good family, I must start by building a good me. Before I can build a good company, a good department, a good division, or a good team, I must start by building a good me.

That's where the Plus One concept can make all the difference.

## *From Mediocrity to Greatness*

Perhaps you are successful at your job, but you're starting to realize that success isn't the same as significance.

It's not enough to be able to do what your boss expects of you anymore. It's not enough to be scraping by financially or having an amiable marriage. You're ready for significance. You're done with mediocrity and an average, ordinary life.

You're ready for greatness!

Sometimes I go for a run. I hate running. I know there are people who love running, but I'm not one of them. I see the benefits of running, but I don't enjoy it at all. So, when I go for a run, I push myself until I tire. Then I tell myself that I'll run past one more mailbox, one more streetlight, one more block. As I make each goal, I push myself to do one more, and one more after that. I figure that if running until you're tired is what average people do, then one more is what makes people great. I'm not satisfied with mediocrity.

I worked with a young woman who wanted to compete in Miss Kentucky USA a few years back. She'd never competed in this sort of thing before and wasn't sure what training routine would be best, so she came to me. I asked her how many reps she thought the other contestants were doing. She thought about it and came up with the number ten. I said, "Okay, so if the person who comes in tenth place does ten reps, then the person in ninth place does plus one, the person in eighth place does one more than that, and so on."

We used that mindset to help her compete. She came back to me after her very first competition and told me she won third place!

The judges were amazed at her conditioning for her first event, and one even said that she probably would have won first place except that her tan wasn't as dark as some of the other girls'. "I should have done plus one with the spray tan, too," she laughed.

Don't be satisfied with mediocrity. Always strive to do one more. Holding tight to the concept of Plus One will move you toward greatness.

## *A Few Warnings*

Sometimes fear of failure is what stops a person from grabbing hold of the concept of Plus One.

Fear comes in many different packages. You might be afraid to go to the gym and workout because you fear the opinions of the people who are there and already in great shape.

You might fear spending time in prayer because you don't know what you'll say to God or what He will say to you.

You might be afraid to start saving money because then that money won't be available when you see something you want to buy.

You might be afraid of giving up your comfort.

You might fear putting yourself out there because you might get rejected.

But here's an important thing to remember: you already know what life is like when you *don't* do Plus

One. You're living it right now. Are you happy with it? If you've made it this far in the book, I'm guessing that the answer is no.

So, what are you going to lose by adding one more push-up? By spending one more minute with your family? By paying one extra dollar on your credit card bill?

## Excellence Isn't Perfection

If you start a Plus One routine, there will be days when you will mess up. Don't be discouraged!

Say you added one more glass of water each day, and on day ten you gave in and drank a soda instead. It would be easy to throw your hands up, decide that you are a big failure, and go back to where you started. Sadly, people tend to look at their failures more than their successes.

Always remember: *excellence isn't perfection*. You will make mistakes—guaranteed.

We've already spent a chapter on this, but it's worth repeating here. The problem with a perfection mindset is that it makes people slaves. No one can be perfect. It's impossible. A person might spend their entire life desiring perfection, but they will never achieve it. Being excellent, however, allows for failure. It expects the inevitable mistakes and weaknesses.

Striving for excellence looks at that failure and tries to figure out why it happened and what can be done to get back on track.

Suppose you went ten days without buying anything online, and then you went to Amazon and ordered something you absolutely didn't need. Why did that happen? Were you bored? Feeling down? Next time you feel that way, who can you call or text for support so you don't mess up again?

## One Day at a Time

Once I was stuck on the side of a mountain. I was training in free climbing, which is rock climbing without the assistance of devices (such as pegs) while still using ropes and belays occasionally. Halfway to the top of that mountain, I froze. My instructor said, "John, what's going on? You have to keep climbing! You are too big for me to carry, and we're not calling you a helicopter. So if you let go, you're going to fall three hundred feet!"

I was tired. My hands were cramping, and my muscles hurt. There was a long way to go to the top, and I wanted to quit. I was in excruciating pain. I told my instructor all my excuses. He said, "Focus on what you can control in this place right here. Where's the next handhold? Right there, grab it. Okay, where's your next foothold? Right there, take it."

I made it to the top by taking it one handhold and one step at a time. Sometimes I had to go sideways. Sometimes I had to go back down a step. Eventually I made it to the top by focusing on my specific goal one moment at a time.

You can't change your past or control what is going to happen tomorrow. You are only guaranteed today, so you need to focus on this one moment. What can you reasonably do in this moment that will better your life and the lives of those around you?

Remember to focus on your unstoppable "whys" and find the next handhold. Grab it and move that one little bit forward. Even if it's messy, even if you make a mistake, keep moving forward.

If you do Plus One for ten days, you will have added so much to your life. Let's add it up: $1 + 2 + 3 + 4 + 5 + 6 + 7 + 8 + 9 + 10$. The total is fifty-five.

After ten days, you will have read an extra fifty-five Bible verses, done fifty-five more push-ups, had fifty-five more minutes of quality time with your kids, or replaced fifty-five jelly beans with carrots.

There's no way you can look at that and say it's completely insignificant and has had no effect on you.

I hope you've begun to catch a vision of what your life could be, who you want to become, and things that you know need to change. However, you no doubt understand that having the vision of your end goal and arriving at that end goal are two very different things.

The idea of everything necessary to reach your goals can be so overwhelming that you might be tempted either to stay planted on the couch or, conversely, to jump into a completely new lifestyle prematurely.

But remember that Plus One changes everything— one day at a time.

## The Right "Why" and the Right People

It's also important to have the right "why" when you're doing Plus One. It isn't a competition, nor is it an idol that should rule your life.

Making accomplishments about being superior to others, or basing accomplishments on fear will take an unhealthy hold on your life. Wanting to lose weight so that you are healthier and can better play with your kids is an unstoppable "why." Wanting to lose weight because you fear that other people think you are fat is an *unhealthy* "why."

Completing your Plus One for the day is a good step forward, but not completing it isn't a reason to beat yourself up or feel like a failure. Your value is not in completing this Plus One or even reaching the end goal.

Your life is not going to magically change because you have ten thousand dollars in the bank. That goal itself isn't why you're doing it. It's a stepping stone to improving the lives of the people around you.

Finding a Plus One accountability partner is paramount. You will experience moments of weakness, and having someone to call and talk to can mean the difference between pushing forward and giving up. Sometimes you just need that climbing instructor to talk you through the times when you want to quit.

It's also beneficial to have another person identify reasons you failed, and to brainstorm together ways to learn from these failures.

Intentionality is key. You can't pick something halfheartedly, form no plan, and expect results. Choose one area where you want to see results. Then think of how you could add Plus One in that area.

Find an accountability friend, tell this person what you're going to do, and invite them to check in on you daily. Make a specific plan. When will you do this thing? How will you remind yourself to do it?

I've mentioned before how important it is to be aware of the people in your life who are "negative Nancys" (or "Neds"). Prepare for those who may discourage you.

You're all pumped up and motivated, and you tell this friend who responds, "That's stupid. Why are you doing that? What's the point? You're just going to fail."

I've found an interesting thing about the people in my life.

The people who feed my Plus One ask me questions about it. They want to know more, they check in with me, and they ask how I'm feeling each day. On the other hand, people who drain my Plus One give me their opinion without listening to the whole story. They're busier giving me their thoughts about my life than hearing what's actually happening in my life. If you can, keep your distance from these people.

## Baby Steps

Trying to change everything at once is not only overwhelming, but impossible.

One simple change can shift the whole trajectory of your life. So start small—take baby steps. Doing so will move you from mediocrity to greatness, and help prepare you to be the best version of yourself when things are out of your control.

## *Free Download!*

**How To Be A Real Influencer**

*Get my free report on the simple hacks you can use every day to make you more influential at http://expectgreatnesstoday.com/get-bonuses.*

WORKBOOK

# Chapter 7 Questions

**Question:** Building the best you starts with you. What is one aspect of your physical, financial, or social life that needs improvement? What is a specific Plus One you will start today to grow in this area?

_____

_____

_____

_____

_____

_____

_____

_____

_____

_____

_____

**Question:** What is one aspect of your spiritual, emotional, or mental life that needs improvement? What is a specific Plus One you will start today to grow in this area?

_____

_____

_____

_____

_____

_____

_____

_____

_____

_____

**Question:** Who could be your accountability partner? What daily and weekly routines would help you keep in touch with this person?

_____

_____

_____

_____

_____

_____

_____

_____

_____

_____

**Action:** In moving from mediocrity toward greatness, remember to take small steps—baby steps. Begin by committing to one month of Plus One and experience the difference for yourself:

1. Consider the following areas: physical, spiritual, emotional, financial, social, and mental. Which of these do you see as needing some changes? If there's more than one, which one do you think you can do the most easily? Remember, when you start Plus One, it's okay to start small. You aren't competing against anyone, and being successful will give you momentum.

2. Think about one specific thing you can do. Plus One doesn't mean that you have to start at zero. If you're already spending twenty minutes with your spouse at dinner, add one more minute each day. If you're already drinking sixteen ounces of water a day, add one more ounce daily. It's okay to start with one. Maybe you've struggled with reading your Bible for years. Finding an app that sends you a verse a day is a great place to start. Maybe the next day, look that verse up in your Bible and read the verse that comes after it, then two verses, then three, and so on. Decide when you are going to do your Plus One. Arrange your schedule so you can make it happen, if need be. Be intentional and specific.

3. Find an accountability friend. It's easier if this person is also doing a Plus One because he or she will be going through the same thing and will be more mindful of it. Form a plan for when you'll check in on each other each day.

4. Write out your goal. Put it on an index card and tape it to your bathroom mirror, your computer monitor, or your steering wheel. Find a notebook and keep track of your progress each day. Keep a tally of your total to help you see how much you've done. If you mess up, write yourself an encouraging note for that day or ask your accountability partner to write one for you.

# *Chapter 7 Notes*

CHAPTER EIGHT

# Be the Diamond

Geologists and scientists disagree over how diamonds are made. There are vast opinions about how long they take to form and what the exact recipe is. However, these experts do agree on the basics of the process:

Diamonds begin as carbon deep in the earth. The carbon is heated to extreme temperatures and put under enormous pressure. Over a long period of time, this common carbon slowly transforms to rare diamonds.

Think of your life as an opportunity to be a diamond.

You see, it isn't the good times that shape a person, it's the hard times. The times of high heat and extreme pressure are what make or break people. Each person on earth will deal with difficult times. Some people crack, and some shine.

Nelson Mandela is one of those people who chose to shine. He was put into a horrible prison unjustly where he remained for twenty-seven years. Eighteen of those years were spent in a hard-labor prison camp. He saw his wife about once every six months. His five-foot by five-foot cell didn't even have a bed. Most people in those circumstances would have given up, but Nelson Mandela allowed the intense pressure to turn him into a diamond.

He went on to be president of South Africa and made historic changes to the racially divided country.

Let's say you've crafted your personal creed and you're doing your Plus One every day. You are living the dash and expecting greatness. In other words, you're doing everything you can reasonably do to go from survival to success, and from significance to legacy.

Then along comes life, and it runs you over.

If there's anything that can be said about life, it's that it is unexpected. You can only plan so much. I've heard it said, "If you want to make God laugh, tell Him your five-year plan." Stuff happens no one can predict. It knocks you around and leaves you changed and scarred.

It would be unreasonable for me to go through this whole book telling you what *you* must do to change your life without discussing things that happen that you can't control. After all, unanticipated trials or difficulties will come—no one is immune.

So the best thing I can do for you is help you prepare your mind and your heart for when the unexpected happens. I can encourage you to adopt this key attitude: When circumstances try to crush you, don't succumb to the pressure. Instead, become a diamond.

## *Cubic Zirconia*

Now, most people would like to say that they're diamonds. When things are going well, it's easy to picture far-off troubles and envision coming through them with flying colors.

The reality is that it doesn't take much to reveal most people are cubic zirconia—fake diamonds.

Step into a scenario with me:

It's the middle of the night when a big thunderstorm rolls in. The dog is terrified, and your daughter wakes up crying. While you're trying to calm them down, you realize water is coming through one of the closed windows. You find towels and try to keep the damage to a minimum.

That's an example from my real life. It happened a few months back, in fact. I like to think I'm a diamond, but the night of that storm I cracked big time. I'm embarrassed to admit, but I lost my temper and ended up yelling at everyone.

My daughter and our dog finally went to sleep around three in the morning. I was up a lot longer, thinking about why I wasn't acting like a diamond. It wasn't hard to figure out what needed to change. Could I change the rain? Nope. Could I change my daughter's crying? Nope. Could I change the dog? Nope. The water coming through the window? Nope. I couldn't change any of those things.

The only thing I could change was me.

When things get rough, well-developed people are like diamonds. They don't break under pressure, they don't lose their value, and they continue to sparkle regardless of the situation they are in. They don't whine and complain and blame others.

Instead, they take responsibility where they can and strive to be a benefit to everyone around them.

## *Polishing the Diamond*

Diamonds don't come out of the ground looking the way they do in the jewelry store. They must first be cleaned and cut, and the only thing that can cut a diamond is another diamond.

The largest diamond ever found was the Cullinan Diamond in 1905. The man who was asked to cut it spent six months planning how he would do it. We must take note of this.

Being the diamond means constantly looking for personal imperfections as well as strengths. It means focusing on eliminating those imperfections and strengthening assets. It means learning about who you really are rather than who you perceive yourself to be. After all, you can't cut a diamond if you don't know it inside and out.

Being a diamond means focusing on building your strengths. It's easy to concentrate on your flaws, and sometimes that may be all you see—but that isn't who you really are.

Ignoring your strengths is a surefire way to become cubic zirconia. When things get rough, contemplate the situation and focus on your strengths. Your best you will shine forth.

Striving to be the diamond is not easy. Most people are okay with being cubic zirconia because becoming a diamond is difficult. I sure felt like a fake diamond the night of that rain storm. But I chose to be the diamond the next day. I went to my daughter, explained that I had been in a bad mood, and apologized. She went from being tired from lack of sleep and hurt that I'd been so uncaring the night before to feeling protected and precious.

It wasn't easy to humble myself to my little girl, but the value I added to her day was enormous.

## *The Pig Manure*

It's crucial to be the diamond when you're dropped in the middle of a mess you did not ask for or create. I call these messes the "pig manure" of life.

When a diamond is dropped into pig manure, it doesn't lose its value, even though it may be hidden from sight. In the same way, guard against letting circumstances define who you are or how you act.

You may be covered in manure, but you can still be a diamond. No amount of manure will ever change the value of a real diamond. Once that diamond is found and cleaned off, it's as good as new.

All people wind up in pig manure at some point or another. It can be working for a demeaning boss, a living situation you dislike, hard financial times, or a life-changing illness. Sometimes you may even wander into pig manure willingly. If you have cracks and flaws, then when you're dropped in the mess, the filth will become deeply entrenched in your life.

Being the diamond isn't about one moment in time. It's about incredible excellence being built over a lifetime. So seek out and apply wisdom gained from experiences.

As I've said again and again, it takes motivation at the deepest level. Diamonds aren't valuable to themselves. A diamond never improves its own existence by selling itself at an auction and pocketing the cash. Rather, diamonds improve the lives of those around them.

## *Spotting a Diamond*

Gina was a ten-year-old girl I met in Nicaragua. She was living in La Chureca, the largest garbage dump in Central America. It's also home to more than one thousand people who live there in the dump.

When I first met her, she brought me little cups of water because it was hot. Every day, Gina would walk two hours from La Chureca to the church where the ministry team worked. She never said much, but she served the whole team every chance she got.

One day I gave Gina some food. That little girl shared it with the other kids who lived near her rather than eat it herself. Gina was dropped into an incredible amount of pig manure, but she remained a diamond regardless of her circumstances. She was shaped by time and pressure, and the manure pile she was living in didn't change her character.

Another example of a diamond brightly shining is my friend, Donny, who was an executive at a company he helped to start. Donny gave money to the owner when the company started. The owner said, "We'll always be partners, Donny. We'll be doing this 50-50."

When the company was sold, the official owner took home $30 million. Donny took home $1 million.

The original money he'd loaned his friend had been repaid without interest. I know that Donny was tempted to become bitter. However, he realized he couldn't change anything in that situation except his own attitude. Against everything that the world would probably tell him, he chose to be thankful rather than jealous.

Here's one more example: I met a girl named Christina who was going places. She was an incredible athlete and had a dream to become a combat medic in the Army. One day her knee popped out of the socket. She recovered, but during her training for the Army, it happened again. She couldn't continue.

For a while Christina fought depression. Her dreams had come crashing down around her. She even made some foolish choices because of that depression. Then, in spite of the pig manure that she fell into and the pig manure she walked into willingly, Tina realized she wasn't where she wanted to be.

She pulled herself up and pressed on, following new dreams. She eventually married a veterinarian, and the two of them are foster parents. Tina had the choice to do something about her life. She had to choose to master her thoughts, then her beliefs, then her actions, and then her habits. She chose to go from survival to success to significance.

That is excellence, my friend. That is greatness.

## *Becoming the Diamond*

This book is all about expecting greatness from yourself and those around you. Every chapter was written to help you on your way toward excellence. As you commit to making changes toward greatness, embrace these reminders:

First, don't be discouraged when the goals you want to reach take time.

You spent five years building that credit card debt. It's not going to disappear overnight. Maybe you have a problem with drugs or alcohol. Programs for recovering addicts have a lot of steps and take years to be considered successful. Addictions take hold of people and don't want to let go. Be patient with your recovery. If you start making any sort of changes to your life, your family is going to be surprised and maybe even skeptical. Let them have time to adjust.

Secondly, being intentional is critical.

You can read this whole book and put it on the shelf and not make a single change. You must put each step into action. Give it lots of thought, but give it lots of action, too. If you start something and realize you want to course correct, that's okay. It's better to stand up and take a step than to sit still thinking about it and never doing it.

Finally, diamonds need other diamonds. They cannot cut themselves.

It's vital to find people who are being excellent and draw close to them. These are the people who will encourage you and keep you accountable. There are going to be a lot of cubic zirconia around who don't care if you ever become a diamond. They will never help you become your best self. Those friends and acquaintances who are pulling you away from greatness need to be removed from your life. Stay aware of who is building you and who is piling on the pig manure—and cut ties if necessary.

I hope and pray that you choose to become the diamond. The value you could add to the lives of the people around you could be world changing.

The pressure and extreme heat of this world might crack you, but it can also turn you into a diamond.

The choice is up to you.

# *Free Download!*

## How To Be A Real Influencer

*Get my free report on the simple hacks you can use every day to make you more influential at http://expectgreatnesstoday.com/get-bonuses.*

# Chapter 8 Questions

**Question:** What circumstances have helped define you or influence how you act? If you are honest, would you consider yourself a diamond or a cubic zirconia pretending to be a diamond? Why?

_____

_____

_____

_____

_____

_____

_____

_____

_____

_____

_____

**Question:** In what ways do you strive to be a diamond? What additional changes could help make this transformation a reality?

_____

_____

_____

_____

_____

_____

_____

_____

_____

_____

_____

**Question:** What examples of diamonds do you have in your life that will keep you motivated?

_____

_____

_____

_____

_____

_____

_____

_____

_____

_____

**Action:** Commit to making changes toward greatness! Find people who are already being excellent and draw close to them. Don't get discouraged when you don't reach your goals overnight, but consistently take specific action toward becoming a diamond.

## *Chapter 8 Notes*

CHAPTER NINE

# How to Change the World in Three Simple Steps

"Save the cheerleader, save the world."

That tagline from the first season of the TV show *Heroes*, simultaneously reassuring and daunting in its simplicity, boiled down a complex narrative into a clear, one-step recipe for world salvation.

While none of us is likely to save the world—and if we did, it probably would not hinge on rescuing a cheerleader—each of us is entirely capable of *changing* the world in a few simple steps.

There are three foundational and uncomplicated steps to change the world, which I'll describe at their most basic level. These steps have been proven over thousands of years. They are extremely important, and their application will take lots of hard work.

These three simple steps take incredible sacrifice and ongoing attention. Don't be fooled into thinking that 'simple' means 'easy,' or you will have a hard time putting these steps into action. Being a diamond sometimes involves muddling through difficult, intense times. It takes work, but if you long to make a difference in this world—if you desire personal greatness—work is necessary.

And the result will be worth your toil. Committing to these three steps will make a difference in your life, your family, in your community—and ultimately, in the world.

## *Choose Faith*

The first step to changing the world is exercising faith.

Now, because faith isn't tangible, it confuses a lot of people. It's related to belief and hope, and it's sometimes connected to religion, yet the very essence of faith runs much deeper.

I define faith as complete confidence in something or someone.

In a sense, faith is an investment in your future. It's choosing certain actions now that you believe will pay off in the future.

Have faith, first, in yourself. You may be aware of certain changes you need to make, but don't have faith that you'll be successful. You may think, "I've failed at every exercise program I've tried, so why bother with a new one?" or "I'm not good at school, so I'm not going to go back and try to finish my degree."

Faith in yourself is a tenuous thing. Years of bad habits and negative opinions may be weighing on you. If you muscle up the courage to try something new, one punch may take you down for the count.

That's the exact reason faith in others is so important. You cannot get through this life without other people. It's an enormous risk to reach out and start building relationships, especially when you've been burned by people in the past.

I keep mentioning the importance of letting go of certain relationships, and I'll say it again here. You cannot build healthy trust in people when you have ongoing friendships that are sabotaging your faith in people. One friend who tears you down will affect all your friendships. Let go of the people who are breaking you down, and wisely pursue friendships with people who will encourage you.

Have faith in trusted friends and have faith in yourself. Be discerning of where and in whom you place your faith, as it will be what carries you through rocky times.

### *Cling to Hope*

Though faith is critical and will be what upholds you in trials, accept the fact that storms are a part of life, both literally and figuratively. When the chips are down and you are facing one of life's hurricanes, the only thing that will bring you through is hope. Hope is the feeling of expectation and the desire for a specific thing to happen.

Depression is the exact opposite of hope and is so very damaging because it forces people to live in a state of hopelessness. How can a person walk day by day through a battering rain unless he or she has hope that it will come to an end?

Hope is a tricky thing. It comes from so many different places that it's hard to pinpoint one specific source. You may hope that an illness will come to an end, that your boss will see the effort you've put in and promote you, or that the time and effort you put in to your family will produce stronger people.

Hope is the goal, the best-case scenario, the dream you cling to.

It's also often dependent on others.

If I'm hoping that I will get in shape, the action to reach that goal lies mainly with me. It's a different kind of hope from the hope I have that my business will prosper or I'll meet the person I want to be with for the rest of my life. Hope that depends on other people is scary and delicate. It's also stronger and more life giving than hope that depends only on one's self.

When the storm comes, other people can provide hope to hang on to when you're out of strength. Hope will give you a reason to live when you would rather give up.

Again, if you don't have relationships with people who will support you when life becomes scary, you might not have the hope you need to weather the storm.

## *Embrace Love*

I've had people disagree with me about faith and hope, but no one ever argues that it's impossible to be successful in life without love.

Love is such an overused word, isn't it? People may "love" a show, "love" a workout, or "love" a restaurant. You might even say you love people when you really don't. This culture has become so used to the word 'love' that its true meaning is lost.

The best description of love that I know comes from a well-known portion of the Bible called the "Love Chapter." First Corinthians 13:4–7 says:

> Love is patient, love is kind. It does not envy, it does not boast, it is not proud. It does not dishonor others, it is not self-seeking, it is not easily angered, it keeps no record of wrongs. Love does not delight in evil but rejoices with the truth. It always protects, always trusts, always hopes, always perseveres. **(NIV)**

Now, you might disagree with me here and point out one or two things that you feel don't describe love. What I want to point out is that each description of love in this Scripture passage is about what love *does*. Love is an action word.

Without action, in fact, love isn't love. If I tell my wife I love her and then never help her around the house or ask her how she's feeling, do I really love her? Possibly, but I guarantee you that my wife doesn't feel my love. How can I love my friends if I never have time to spend with them? Love requires action.

And the deepest love requires extraordinary action.

Think of what parents do to keep their children safe. Think of the sacrifices our military makes on a daily basis to protect freedoms and loved ones. Think of what real friends do for a friend who is terminally ill with cancer. There are so many great quotes about love, and one of my favorites is John 15:13: "Greater love has no one than this: to lay down one's life for one's friends"(NIV).

Love is more than something a person enjoys or likes. It is active and intentional. When you choose to take the step to love others well, you will profoundly impact the world—one person at a time.

## *My Storm*

In September of 2016, Hurricane Matthew hit the United States. My family lived in Florida at the time, just a few miles from the beach. The weather reports announced that it was going to be a terrible storm, and word spread that mandatory evacuations were going to start soon.

I called a friend who lived out of the path of the hurricane and asked if my wife, daughter, and dog could stay with him. Then I started to prepare my house for the storm.

I brought everything inside that would be in danger of blowing away. I prepared the windows, and I bought supplies. In fact, I was so well prepared that I was ready before most of my neighbors started their preparations.

With time on my hands, I went around helping other people secure their homes for the storm.

My friend at the National Oceanic and Atmospheric Administration (NOAA) called and told me that the storm was going to be much worse than newscasters were letting on.

Then the storm hit and I learned he wasn't kidding. The winds were strong enough to shake my cinderblock house, knock over fence posts, and uproot trees.

In the middle of the storm, while it was still going strong, I heard a banging outside. I went to my window and saw that my ninety-two-year-old neighbor, Joe, was having some trouble. The storm shutters he was using to protect his windows had come loose and were banging against the house. He had cut a hole in the window screen and was holding the shutters closed with one hand through one-hundred-mile-per-hour winds and rain.

I opened my window and called out to him.

Joe gave me a thumbs up to let me know he was okay, but I worried about him. Every thirty minutes or so, I would open my window and call out encouragement to him. Finally, after eight long hours, the wind died down enough that Joe could let go of his shutters and get some rest.

The next day we had to assess the damage. There was debris everywhere, trees were down, and shingles had been ripped off houses. Every able person got to work cleaning our yards and helping the people around us. A young man I know named Brandon came from across town and lent a hand just because he knew me and wanted to help.

## Three Steps in Action

That storm clarified the importance of faith, hope, and love for me. It started with me putting my faith to work. I had faith and utmost confidence that my friend would take care of what was most precious to me: my family. I had faith that my meteorologist friend was correct and the storm was going to be bad, and I didn't waste time getting my preparations done. I had faith that helping my neighbors with their storm prep was worth my time and effort.

Then the storm hit, and I exercised hope that the storm would eventually pass. Joe needed hope in the form of my encouragement through the eight hours he held that shutter. After the storm was over, he told me that my checking on him every half hour was what carried him through the long hours. I had given Joe hope. He looked forward to each time I would call out to him, knowing that I would be there again in another half hour. He knew he wasn't alone and that if the storm escalated, there was someone who would be there for him.

When the storm itself dissipated and everyone was left to deal with the aftermath, our love for each other started to show. We worked tirelessly for about twenty hours straight to clear away the worst of the debris and to make sure our neighbors slept peacefully that night. I felt loved by Brandon, who came to help me. He even went on to help other people because he knew it would make their lives better.

These three things—faith, hope, and love—are absolutely the most important character traits that will drive you to success in your business, your community, your marriage, and your family. Faith, hope, and love are what take a person from good to great to awesome and from survival to success to significance to legacy. They are the deepest motivations behind your unstoppable "whys."

I've been noticing lately how little faith, hope, and love the news media covers. The presidential election between Hillary Clinton and Donald Trump left much of America feeling like neither candidate was a good choice. Many had no faith, no hope, and no love for either candidate, which left people feeling hopeless when they looked to the future of this country.

When the June 2016 nightclub shooting happened in Orlando, hours of footage ran across people's television sets revealing the hatred that caused the shooting. But only a few minutes of the extraordinary love that poured out for the victims was covered.

You see, a gunman opened fire at a gay nightclub. Everyone heard about that. What wasn't reported on extensively was how the citizens of Orlando and the rest of the world responded to that shooting by donating blood to the Red Cross. There were people who waited in line for hours to give blood to show their support for the victims.

Faith, hope, and love aren't flashy responses to trials, and they certainly are not going to sell newspapers. People who remain faithful, cling to hope, and love others are unglamorous. Often they are the real, unsung heroes.

When you cut through all the mess, noise, confusion, and chaos of life, you will find that faith, hope, and love will carry you through the storms of life and empower you to live a life of excellence and greatness.

As you're reading this book, you need to start making some decisions about your life. Start cutting out some people who don't belong there. Rid yourself of negativity that you've accepted as being okay. Let go of the people who speak junk, mess, noise, and confusion into your life, and surround yourself with people who are full of faith, hope, and love. You don't want to face your next defeat with somebody who will rub your nose in it. Nor do you want to celebrate your victory with people who won't rejoice with you.

Go back to your Plus One. Today make a choice to do one more thing that will demonstrate faith in others or build faith in yourself.

It's time to act and begin to show love to yourself and others, and have hope in your future.

Though your past can help you know what pitfalls to avoid, stop holding on to guilt and shame. Your mistakes happened. Learn from them, and move on.

Become a firm believer in how you can impact the world by having faith, holding tight to hope, and loving others. Doing so will make a difference in your life, your family, your community—and ultimately, the world.

## *Free Download!*

### How To Be A Real Influencer

*Get my free report on the simple hacks you can use every day to make you more influential at http://expectgreatnesstoday.com/get-bonuses.*

WORKBOOK

# Chapter 9 Questions

**Question:** To what extent do you have faith (or not) in your life now? In what particular ways can faith help you have a better future?

_____

_____

_____

_____

_____

_____

_____

_____

_____

_____

_____

**Question:** What are the sources of hope in your life?

_____

_____

_____

_____

_____

_____

_____

_____

_____

_____

_____

**Question:** How can you make more time in your life to spend time with your family, friends, and others who need your love?

_____

_____

_____

_____

_____

_____

_____

_____

_____

_____

**Action:** Remain a firm believer in your ability to impact the world! Follow the simple three-step plan: (1) having faith, (2) holding tight to hope, and (3) loving others. By following these steps on a daily basis, embrace your capacity to make a real difference in your life, your family, your community, and the world.

# *Chapter 9 Notes*

CONCLUSION

# Never Give Up

*Let us not become weary in doing good, for at the proper time we
will reap a harvest if we do not give up.*
—*Galatians 6:9 (NIV)*

Where have you landed, after reading this book?

Perhaps you have not done a single thing I've
recommended. Perhaps you tried a few ideas, and
skipped others. Or you may have done everything I've
told you to do.

No matter which of these scenarios describes you, I
must warn you: you are going to face the desire to give
up.

It will be tempting to give up if you've never started.
You might see the fact that you haven't done anything as
a sign that you're going to fail if you ever do give this
book a shot. If you've tried some or all I have
recommended, the time is going to come when you will
make a mistake or have a bad day, and you'll start
wondering if it's worth it to keep fighting.

## *Don't Give Up*

Life is hard. Everyone seems to know this in theory, but are still shocked by the reality of it. There's that old saying by Benjamin Franklin, "Nothing is certain except death and taxes." They are certainties, but people are still amazed when they continue to come around.

I often tell people that they're only human and mistakes are inevitable. At the same time, I am always struggling to forgive myself when I mess up.

Develop a mindset that says, "Hey, when things get tough, I'm going to get tougher." You might just be hanging on by a finger and barely surviving, but eventually you will come through the hard times and will thrive.

When you have a Never Give Up mindset, you take the hard things and use them to make yourself stronger, better, and faster. You take the knowledge and experience you've gained by walking through hard times and walk away with wisdom.

### The Wrong Reason

There are two kinds of people with the Never Give Up mindset. The first kind is people who refuse to quit for their own benefit. They don't give up because they want to be better than everyone else, to have their own needs met above all else, and to show off their first-place trophies. You know you're dealing with one of these people if they're willing to sacrifice anything to get whatever it is they think they deserve. They often have no ethics because they don't care if others are hurt so long as they reach the top.

This kind of motivation is going to contribute to a Never Give Up mindset, that's for sure. However, it's an empty, lonely way to go. When you're willing to sacrifice everyone around you to reach the top, you will arrive to find you're all alone.

Maybe there are people living in your house or working in your office or going to get drinks with you, but they'll leave you stranded the minute things become difficult. Though you may be super successful, you'll never be significant, and you'll never leave a legacy you will be proud of. Eventually you will realize that you worked your whole life for things that you can't take with you.

I was in a business with a guy named Mike. He and I were going to be vendors for a company that guaranteed us an enormous return on our profits. We had to station our business on solid ground and have a large amount of money in the bank before the other company would start to work with us. You see, it was going to take some hard work before we could start turning this huge profit, and the other company needed us to be financially solid and stable.

The months went by, and Mike and I were working to elevate our business to the right place. It took a lot longer than we'd expected.

Finally, the day came when the executives from the other company came to sign the paperwork. They looked everything over and were happy with what they saw. I was so excited finally to get the ball rolling. We sat down in the office, ready to sign the paperwork. When I made the call to the bank to get our official statement of finances in our accounts, I was shocked to hear the banker tell me there was nothing in the account.

I couldn't believe it!

It turns out that Mike had gotten tired of waiting. The day before the other company called to set up this meeting, he went to the bank, withdrew all the money, and took off. The *day* before the other company called! If Mike had waited *one more day* before he quit, we would have been set for life financially.

The other company backed out of the deal since I couldn't meet my end of the bargain to show adequate finances in our accounts. There was no time to raise the money again. They had to go with their second-choice vendor. I had to tell the people working for us that not only were they out of work, but I couldn't pay them for that week, either.

Mike was a partner in our business, yet he was in business for himself. When he gave up, he hurt dozens of people and their families. There was no reason why he needed that much money at that moment in time. He simply grew tired of waiting. He elevated himself over everyone else and moved on to something that would benefit him.

If he'd only come to me and said he wanted out, we could have found a healthy way for him to leave.

## The Right Reason

The only motivation that is going to move you through the levels toward significance is other people. This is the motivation that helps someone stick with a marriage when their spouse cheats. Now, I'm not saying every spouse should stay in a marriage that has infidelity. However, there are situations where the marriage is still salvageable. It would be easy to file for divorce, and no one would fault that person. It's incredibly more difficult to stay and find out whether the marriage can survive or not.

I've mentioned before that my dad died when I was seven. My mom worked three jobs, and we lived in a trailer park. Where we lived, there were several kids I played with who had the same little old Mexican grandmother, Abuelita. I loved going over to play with them. There was always a small group of us there.

However, Abuelita had a habit of getting out her broom and chasing other kids away. Again and again these kids would come over to play, and Abuelita would chase them away with her broom, yelling at them in Spanish. At first I didn't understand what she was doing, but then one day it clicked for me. Those kids were a rough group. They already had ties to gangs and were into some bad stuff. Abuelita tirelessly fought to keep them away from influencing her grandchildren. She wouldn't quit protecting us because she wanted to give us a chance to be free from gangs.

I can't encourage you enough to get out an index card and write down why you are fighting through this life.

There's something about writing things down that makes them powerful and concrete in our lives. When you are faced with a decision or one of life's gut punches, you can look to that card and use it to keep yourself on track.

I'll tell you my reason for never quitting.

I exist to make an impact on the people God has put in my life. That's why I have the Never Give Up mindset. I've written this down, and when life throws me a curveball—when I face bankruptcy because my partner quit, when I must do something that's going to be incredibly painful—I look at that card and remember why I won't give up. It helps me make choices that are in line with my purpose for life.

## *Flipping the Switch*

Choosing the Never Give Up mindset is like flipping a switch in your mind. It isn't something that you do halfheartedly. It takes determination and intention.

You might have quit on something before. Okay, that happened already. Are you ready to flip the switch and choose never to give up? It isn't easy. Quitting will always be easier than digging in your heels and sticking it out.

My friend Danny decided to train for one of those crazy-hard obstacle course marathons. This one is called World's Toughest Mudder. It's an event where the contestants complete as many obstacles and run as many miles as possible in twenty-four hours.

Danny trained and trained, and then he trained some more. His goal was to complete fifty miles in the twenty-four hours. The first year he attempted this, he started the course and set off strong, but a severe sandstorm and bone-numbing cold after the water obstacles led him to crawl into his sleeping bag to try and get warm. He never got warm, and after a couple of hours of shivering, he knew he was going to have to make a choice to finish the race or quit. He chose to crawl out of the sleeping bag and struggled unsuccessfully to accomplish his goal.

He tried again the next year with better results. However, it wasn't until his third year that he finally accomplished his goal of fifty miles. It was absolutely incredible to have the drive and determination to attempt that particular race not once, not twice, but three times over three years before accomplishing his goal of fifty miles in twenty-four hours.

As I talked to Danny after the third and successful year, I asked him what motivated him to come back year after year to accomplish (and exceed) his goal.

He said it really came down to the moment the first year when he was freezing and shivering and had to decide to get out of the sleeping bag and do his best to finish the race.

Many thoughts went through his head when he was trying to make the difficult and painful decision to continue on. One key thing that helped drive him forward in that race and for the next two years was a discussion he and I had in which I shared with him that his life was to be a life of no regrets, no retreats, and no surrender.

His goal had been to make it the full twenty-four hours the first year. That didn't happen. Then came time to decide whether to quit or press on. It was one of those life-defining moments when he chose to get up and keep going. His decision carried him through the unsuccessful first and second attempts and finally drove him to victory!

Danny took his life to a whole other level when he flipped that mental switch. He is living proof that when things become tough, we don't stop, we don't quit, and we never give up!

## *Pruning the Tree*

If I were an apple tree, my success would be measured in growing healthy apples. If a branch was dead or diseased, I would need to prune it for the health of the tree.

There will be things that you need to prune from your life if you want a life full of excellence and greatness.

Sometimes shutting down your company so that you can start over is important. You might take a job to make ends meet in the short term, knowing that it is a means to pay bills and not a career. There are probably relationships you need to prune to grow to the next level of excellence.

Here's how I discern if something needs pruning.

First, I go back to my index card and see if the situation is aligned with my life goals. I look at each opportunity to see if I will be able to do things that matter for reasons that matter with people who matter to me. If I'm not making the impact on the right people for the right reasons, I realize that I must prune that opportunity or activity out of my life. It's that simple. Even if the opportunity might make me a millionaire, if it's not in alignment with who I am and what I was created to do, I intentionally and fully prune it from my life.

Secondly, I look at the long term rather than the short term. Second Corinthians 4:18 says, "So we fix our eyes not on what is seen, but on what is unseen, since what is seen is temporary, but what is unseen is eternal" (NIV). This verse teaches that Christians need to keep their eyes on the goal of eternity, not on the problems that pop up in this life.

Even if you're not a Christian, there's a lot of wisdom in this verse.

Achieving a legacy of generosity will take a lifetime of choices and sacrifices.

Achieving a legacy of being an incredible teacher means that you're going to have to fight through thousands of days of work in the trenches with students who don't want to learn.

Want the legacy of a wonderful family? You will have to choose to spend time with your kids daily rather than sitting back and watching TV.

## *Be SMART*

One acronym I use a lot in my life is SMART. You may remember from earlier that SMART stands for specific, measurable, achievable, realistic, and timely. This acronym applies to goals, expectations, and life in general.

Your aims in life should not be random; they should fit you. Never Give Up doesn't mean latching on to ideas for which you're not equipped. I like the phrase, "The need is not the call." Just because there's world hunger doesn't mean you are meant to be the person who has the solution.

Most of the time, the biggest impact you can have in the world results from loving individuals.

When I thank someone for getting out of bed early to make my coffee, I set off a chain of kindness that can touch lives. It's crucial to spend time on things that matter for reasons that matter with people who matter to me. Being a fantastic business man and leader are great goals; however, deeply loving people and sowing into their lives is what will allow me to leave the legacy that I want.

Setting SMART goals and pruning things that aren't in line with those goals allow you to live life without regrets.

When I look toward the end goal, I also understand that I might not see the final effects of my behavior—but I have faith that they are there. Choosing the Never Give Up mindset is a lifelong series of choices that must be made daily. It requires recognition of mistakes and learning from them, and making the commitment to keep going. A Never Give Up mindset will result in a legacy that changes lives.

## *The Right People and the Right Tools*

I know I sound like a broken record. However, I'll say it again: the people around you are key to your success. Surround yourself with people who don't quit. When things get hard and you are tempted to let go, it is critical to have people in your life who will stand next to you and chant, "Don't stop! Don't quit! Never give up!"

When I'm not doing things for the right reasons or I'm giving excuses, I need my support system to say, "John, that's an excuse. Dig your heels in, and stay the course." You will need that kind of support system, too.

Quitters love it when other people quit because it justifies their quitting. *Oh, you gave up because things were too hard? So did I! I guess I made the right choice since I'm not the only one who quit.*

Quitters might survive. They might have good lives. But they will never live significant lives, they will never thrive, and they will have a lifetime of regrets. Success is about me; significance is about others. Quitting is about me; perseverance is about others.

When life punches you in the gut, you must have people who will step in and help you to keep going.

People who have had rocky patches in their marriages can help you work through your marriage challenges.

People who have had businesses fail and found ways to keep going can help you navigate how to care for your business when things grow tough.

People who have made mistakes and pulled themselves back up can help you do the same.

Recall that letter to your younger self: What hard-won lessons have you learned that you would love to teach your younger self? What pain could you have avoided? How could your life be better if you'd only known what you do?

You have a set of tools now to help answer those questions, strive for personal greatness, and make changes that will impact many.

Get your index card and write down your reason for pressing through the hardships of this life. It's time to stop settling for just getting by.

It's time to stand and fight for a life that really means something.

You weren't meant to slog through life or mark time until it's over. Choose to pursue excellence and expect greatness from yourself and those around you!

CALL TO ACTION

# The Next Step

If there was ever a time to differentiate yourself and **stand out from the crowd**, it is *now*! In today's world, where change happens faster than the blink of an eye, people want the proven leadership strategies that will empower them to tackle our crazy 24/7 world so they can:

- Be better leaders.
- Live with Honor, Courage, and Commitment.
- Communicate and connect effectively.
- Love more deeply.
- Stay healthy longer.
- Make more memories along the way.
- And experience more excellence in their lives than they ever thought possible.

I help people grow themselves, their teams and their organizations strategically for maximum success and peak performance.

## *What Others Say*

"John is an out of the box thinker with an IQ ... and EQ ... that is off the charts. It is his ability to incorporate various data points and translate them into something actionable, that moves people and teams in a positive direction."

— **Paul DeSmet, Executive Vice President, LINE-X Protective Coatings**

"I recently had the pleasure to work with John in developing leadership skills in an ever-changing, fast-paced work environment. I have seen my team members respond to his coaching, mentoring, and training and transform into leaders they need to be. John takes the time to learn and understand what your needs are in order to engage people to lead through change."

— **Rosa Pizzuto, Global Supplier Quality Director, Stryker**

## *What Makes Me Different*

No wasted time. No smoke and mirrors. No snake oil.

Just proven methods for increasing execution, effectiveness, and excellence!

# *Specialties*

Coaching
Speaking
Experiential Development
Leadership Assessment
Mastermind Groups
Strategy, Innovation, Reinvention
Hyper Leadership Growth
High-Performance Team Building

I look forward to hearing from you and helping you achieve your highest level of true excellence and greatness!

*— John Hawkins*

Ready to talk?
Email me at jhawkins@buildingeffectiveleaders.com.

**Website:** https://buildingeffectiveleaders.com/
**Twitter:** https://twitter.com/johnhawkins
**Facebook:**
https://www.facebook.com/BuildingEffectiveLeaders
**Linked In:**
https://www.linkedin.com/in/JohnHawkinsBEL

*Motivate. Equip. Transform.*

REFERENCES

# Notes

1.  Gaultiere, Bill. "Fear Not … 365 Days a Year." *Soultransformation*. The Christian Broadcasting Network. 21 October 2011. http://www1.cbn.com/soultransformation/archive/2011/10/21/fear-not.-365-days-a-year
2.  "Perfectionism." *Merriam-Webster*. https://www.merriam-webster.com/dictionary/perfectionism
3.  "Excellence." *English: Oxford Living Dictionaries*. Oxford University Press. https://www.merriam-webster.com/dictionary/perfectionism

# About the Author

John Hawkins is a leadership speaker who knows how to accelerate growth and development effectively for high-performance individuals, teams, and organizations. John imparts leadership strategies and concepts that help empower individuals and thereby add value to their organizations, communities, schools, and lives. Interweaving deep core values and day-to-day actions, John urges us to dive headfirst into a leadership style that Reaches Every Aspect of Life (R.E.A.L) and provides a blueprint for long-term success, significance, and legacy. John Hawkins' universal message of *honor*, *courage*, and *commitment* strongly resonates with a tone of practicality, honesty, and humor.

John Hawkins is a member of Forbes Coaches Council on Leadership and Management and an active member on several boards of directors. His multifaceted work includes:

## Top Leadership Keynote Speaker

As a highly in-demand motivational speaker and thought leader, John Hawkins speaks about leadership at events and conferences across the globe. John Hawkins' thought-provoking message encourages each of us to lead with substance, significance, and success.

## Leadership Coach and Consultant

John Hawkins is a senior-level leadership coach and consultant who has worked with hundreds of clients, large and small, across all sectors. Check out some of the reviews on the website or on Linked In!

## Leadership Author

Beyond his work as an inspirational speaker, John Hawkins has written numerous articles and posts for business magazines and higher education institutions on personal leadership and developing high-performance teams.

John is married to his beautiful wife, Tammy, and has a highly energetic daughter, Sophia. He loves God, his family, and his country. When there's time, he loves to ride his motorcycle or travel the world seeking out new flavors of ice cream and gelatto (over 200 tried so far).

# About Speak It To Book

Speak It to Book is revolutionizing how books are created and used.

Traditional publishing requires thousands of hours, and then you're asked to surrender your rights. Self-publishing is indicative of a poor-quality product with no prestige. And neither model boasts results-driven marketing.

That's why we created a better option. Speak It To Book has the attention of the industry because we are disrupting it in a brilliant way.

Our process:

√ **Establishes you as an authentic thought leader in your market** so you can own prestigious and lucrative space in your niche.

√ **Attracts and acquires your ideal clients/readers** so you can boost your ROI or achieve a specific goal (i.e. speak more nationally, build your online presence, start recurring revenue streams).

√ **Completes your book in less than 24 hours of your time** so you can continue focusing on your current responsibilities and business ventures.

Imagine if you had a way to get those ideas out of your head? If you could get your story in front of the people who need it most? If you took the next step into significance and influence?

You can accomplish all of these goals by writing a book. Plus, you can do it without having to make a single keystroke, and in less than one-hundredth of the time.

Your ideas are meant for a wider audience. So step into significance—by speaking your story into a book.

Visit www.speakittobook.com to learn more.

Made in the USA
Middletown, DE
23 July 2017